KU-267-159

100 ways to understand your DOG

100 ways to understand your
DOG

Roger Tabor

David and Charles

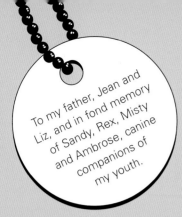

A DAVID & CHARLES BOOK
Copyright © David & Charles Limited 2006

David & Charles is an F+W Publications
Inc. company
4700 East Galbraith Road
Cincinnati, OH 45236

First published in the UK in 2006

Text copyright © Roger Tabor 2006
Photographs copyright © Roger Tabor 2006,
except for those listed on page 143

Roger Tabor has asserted his right to be identified as author
of this work in accordance with the Copyright, Designs and
Patents Act, 1988.

All rights reserved. No part of this publication may be
reproduced, stored in a retrieval system, or transmitted,
in any form or by any means, electronic or mechanical,
by photocopying, recording or otherwise, without prior
permission in writing from the publisher.

A catalogue record for this book is available from the
British Library.

ISBN-13: 978-0-7153-2173-7 paperback
ISBN-10: 0-7153-2173-0 paperback

Printed in China by SNP Leefung
for David & Charles
Brunel House   Newton Abbot   Devon

Commissioning Editor Jane Trollope
Editor Jennifer Proverbs
Assistant Editor Emily Rae
Designer Emma Sandquest
Production Controller Kelly Smith
Project Editor Ian Kearey

Visit our website at www.davidandcharles.co.uk

David & Charles books are available from all good
bookshops; alternatively you can contact our Orderline
on 0870 9908222 or write to us at FREEPOST EX2 110,
D&C Direct, Newton Abbot, TQ12 4ZZ (no stamp required
UK only); US customers call 800-289-0963 and Canadian
customers call 800-840-5220.

The publisher has endeavoured to contact all contributors of
pictures for permission to reproduce.

*While the author and publishers have made every attempt
to offer accurate and reliable information to the best of
their knowledge and belief, it is presented without any
guarantee. The author and publishers therefore disclaim any
liability incurred in connection with using the information
contained in this book.*

Contents

 Thanks to Bella, Working Cocker Spaniel

Man's best friend

As a child I was fortunate to grow up with both dogs and cats. My earliest recollection of a dog was of my grandparents' dog, Rex. He was a 'bitsa' dog – 'bitsa this, bitsa that' – in other words, a mongrel. This term has become one that is used as abuse, yet mongrels or mutts have the genetic vitality of outbreeding. (In the dog world, many owners strive to have identifiable breed dogs, while in the cat world breed cats are the minority and the moggie is the majority.)

Great Dane & Chihuahua

Golden Retriever

When I was a young teenager, my Golden Retriever, Sandy, and I were inseparable. My interest in the natural world was in part fostered by Sandy, for we used to climb the hill behind our home up into the woods and walked for hours, reaching small lakes where Sandy would jump enthusiastically into the water and swim about with the natural prowess of his breed. We attended dog-training classes, and I became pleased with his facility to sit at the kerbside while waiting to cross a road. Later, my younger sister had an elegant Collie, whose long, tapered face gave it a gentle expression set off proudly by its full ruff.

My parents then had a Springer Spaniel called Ambrose, who was always so eager to greet people that he almost wagged his tail off. Yet it was Ambrose who introduced me to canine behaviour problems, for he pulled on his lead when my parents walked their dog; in his excitement to greet he sometimes urinated a little on the floor; and he was fiercely possessive of his seat. I was later to discover the importance of his genetics and upbringing, and, relationship to his owners in shaping his temperament and behaviour.

Regardless of the animals' different characters, each was loved wholeheartedly by their human 'pack'. They were recognized as individuals with individual characters, just as much as if they had been human members of the family – indeed, our dogs, like those of most dog owners, were looked on as 'family'. Our inclination to enrol our pets as family members is natural, for we are fitting them into our framework of our own species behaviour pattern.

Our dogs perceive us as pack members for the same reasons, and it is because they are pack animals that we have had an apparently matter-of-fact relationship with them through history: with the dog's owner as 'pack leader', the dog is always prepared to follow its master. By contrast, our other common pet companion, the more solitary cat, is more tied by its territory, and is less inclined to follow as we walk off. This can be demonstrated by the centre-stage role the dog has played in European art across the last thousand years, accompanying its master on excursions to hunt, while the more independent cat has been included far less frequently. Today there are over 400 dog breeds worldwide, and there is a huge variety of shapes and sizes of the domestic dog (in contrast to the domestic cat); ironically, however, wild dogs (wolves, hunting dogs and so on) are of a narrow, mid-size range, while wild cats vary massively, from tigers to desert cats.

Grey Wolf

Dogs are great companions, and recent research is allowing us to understand them, and their relationship with us, even better.

ABOUT THIS BOOK

Although we may think we know all about our dogs' characters and behaviour, few of us really understand that how today's dog behaves is based on how his forebears lived in packs and hunted for survival – and on the complex relationship with man, which dates back many thousands of years.

The first part of this book, 'Where Dogs Come From', explores the ancestry of the dog, taking in the most important discoveries of the past few years and linking modern, selectively chosen and trained breeds to the more 'primitive', older breeds still to be found across the world.

The next section, 'Breeds', takes a look at the extraordinary variety of dogs, from size and shape to temperament and behaviour patterns. The classifications of the Kennel Club and American Kennel Club are followed as an easy-to-use guide.

'Training the Growing Dog' focuses on the all-important role of ensuring that your dog knows you are the dominant animal in the household and is thus willing to obey your commands for the good of both of you.

In 'Dealing with Problems' both common and not-so-common problems are analysed; solutions and tips are offered, and the part that can be played by canine behaviourists and trainers in helping you and your dog is examined.

The final section, 'Dogs and Us', focuses on the broader spectrum of man's relationship with his best friend, and gives some pointers on the concerns that will continue to engage us in a new millennium.

Little dogtags, shown right, are used throughout the book to identify the breeds shown.

1

Where dogs come from

Grey Wolf
Canus lupus

Dog design

Types of dog began to develop remarkably early in the history of the dog as a species. There is a great range of shapes and sizes and coats, but the essential dog is within them all. The dog has inherited the wolf pack's hierarchical nature, plus the pack hunter's specialized capacity for the sustained running of the chase. Pursuit of prey depended on keen senses, and the dog has mechanisms to leave and interpret scents.

Forward-looking eyes have a hunter's binocular vision, with a wide field of vision to be aware of others in the hunting pack, and good dusk vision.

Upright-eared dogs can swivel their ears to focus sound using 17 muscles, but this ability is largely missing in floppy-eared dogs.

When dry, the outer part of the dog's nose, the nose pad or rhinarium, can be an indication that the dog is unwell, but this also occurs if the surrounding air is warm and dry.

Dogs have a vastly better sense of smell than us, around a million times more effective, depending on the breed.

The muzzle, including the nose pad and whiskers, is the most sensitive area, wired by large numbers of sensory nerves. The whiskers give the dog information on close contact.

The auditory bulla is a resonating chamber below each ear at the base of the skull that can enhance some high-pitched sounds.

The average-sized dog has a bite around six times stronger than the average human; this bone-crunching jaw grip is an inheritance of its hunting ancestry.

Non-retractable claws give grip in continuous running.

Foot pads cushion the feet like a spongy pad, absorbing shock on impact. The pad has enormously thickened skin, the toughest on the body, and the rough surface gives grip. Dogs can detect vibrations in their pads.

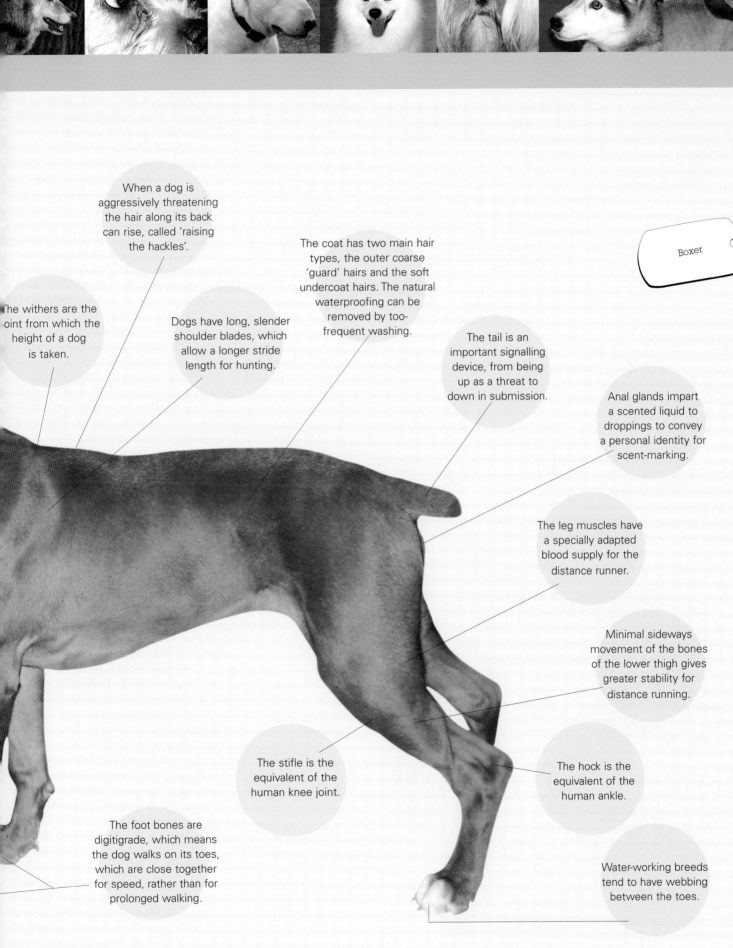

When a dog is aggressively threatening the hair along its back can rise, called 'raising the hackles'.

The coat has two main hair types, the outer coarse 'guard' hairs and the soft undercoat hairs. The natural waterproofing can be removed by too-frequent washing.

The withers are the point from which the height of a dog is taken.

Dogs have long, slender shoulder blades, which allow a longer stride length for hunting.

The tail is an important signalling device, from being up as a threat to down in submission.

Anal glands impart a scented liquid to droppings to convey a personal identity for scent-marking.

The leg muscles have a specially adapted blood supply for the distance runner.

Minimal sideways movement of the bones of the lower thigh gives greater stability for distance running.

The stifle is the equivalent of the human knee joint.

The hock is the equivalent of the human ankle.

The foot bones are digitigrade, which means the dog walks on its toes, which are close together for speed, rather than for prolonged walking.

Water-working breeds tend to have webbing between the toes.

Boxer

1 Origins in the wild

The earliest carnivores appeared in the Eocene period some 50 million years ago and have been called Miacids. While one group that developed from these were the cats and hyenas, another group called the Miacines gave rise to the dog family, along with bears and weasels.

In addition to the wolf, the wild canids include the Jackal, Coyote, Dhole, Bush Dog and African Wild Dog, around 36 species in total. The Hunting Dog is almost as group-oriented and consequently hierarchical in behaviour as the wolf – but not quite; it is the essentially hierarchical nature of the wolf that has made the direct 'leader-and-led' relationship of mankind and the dog possible. Today this close involvement with wolves is still seen in Inuit (Eskimo) settlements in Canada, where crosses occasionally occur between sledge dogs with wolves; selection has to be for not over-fearful or aggressive offspring.

The co-operative hunting of the wolf pack allows animals to catch prey much bigger than themselves; in contrast, the solitary hunting fox is limited to small prey, as its lifestyle is more cat-like due to its woodland habitat.

It is not possible to know when the human/wolf relationship began from archaeological records, just when it had become established. One of the earliest reasonably unambiguous remains comes from a Palaeolithic cave in Iraq from about 12,000 years ago, and is a section of jawbone and teeth (less definitely attributable records may reach back 14,000 years).

Early remains come mainly from West Asia, consistent with early human settlement; they also come from the Americas, Europe, Russia and Japan, as settlement livestock become common in those places. The original distribution of the wolf covered all of these areas, but with such a widespread geographical distribution there was inevitably a range of wolf subspecies.

The wild dogs

Different characteristics in the wolf's ancestry have potentially provided a genetic range of early dogs, rather than a single beginning: for example, the wolves of India and across Asia were smaller than those of Europe and North America.

However, other ancestors, such as the Golden Jackal and Coyote, have been suggested to explain the range of development. These have occasionally produced fertile hybrids with the wolf, as has the domestic dog, so they cannot be ruled out as having formed crosses with the early developing dog. However, due to the far more social nature of the wolf than that of other wild canids, it is usually considered that the wolf is the key, and perhaps the sole ancestor of the dog. There are distinct tooth-pattern differences across the group, and recent DNA evidence also points to the wolf as the prime ancestor.

Indian Pie Dogs

Dogs and man
Co-following by man and wolf hunting herds brought overlap, and wolves scavenging from carcasses would have brought contact. But the biggest change may have occurred when pups were picked up and brought up by people.

Wild relatives: the pack canids

2

The dog family tend to fall into two distinctive groups, separated by food availability and habitat. The first group are the larger canids, the true wolves and African Wild Dogs, who live in packs, allowing them to hunt large prey. The second group comprises the normally smaller canids that feed on smaller prey, including the foxes; these commonly hunt alone and live in pairs or alone.

African Wild Dogs Lycaon pictus

The most social canid is the African Wild Dog, which exists in packs of up to 30 animals that pursue big prey such as zebra and wildebeest. All the pack will regurgitate for the pups of the sole breeding alpha pair – the social canids pack normally only has one breeding pair of dominant animals. They have a 'vocabulary' to keep the pack together involving tail wagging, licking and so on. Juliet Clutton-Brock of the Natural History Museum, London, suggests that regurgitation of food is such a key communication factor amid African Wild Dogs that their communication with people is bound to be limited.

Intriguingly, male pups tend to stay with their original pack, while females move around more into other groups; this is the reverse of most groups of carnivores, including the wolf, where males are more likely to emigrate.

The other pack wild canid is the Dhole of India and South East Asia; these hunt in packs of 5–15 animals, with a group range of around 8 sq km (5 sq m), and are able to overpower Sambar and Chittal deer by group co-operation. They live in areas with dense woodland, which they can pass through in single file, but pursuit and kills are often in the open such as at the water's edge.

I observed the hunt of a pack of Dholes at a lake edge in Kerala, where a large Sambar calf had been separated from its group and forced to go into the water, while the Dhole pack just waited and would not enter the water. The Sambar calf used an unexpectedly effective defence against this group of canids, stamping its foot in the water to splash them – the Dholes stayed back!

3 Wild relatives: foxes, jackals and coyotes

Among the 21 species of fox, with forms as diverse as the Fennec fox, adapted to North African desert life, to the Arctic fox, named after its habitat, the archetypal fox with the most widespread distribution is the Red Fox (left).

Lone hunters of small prey, foxes do not need packs, and most live alone. However, both the Red Fox and the Arctic Fox live as a male and female pair with non-breeding 'helpers' (in the case of the Red Fox, these are females only). They scent-mark their territories with both urine and faeces.

Arctic Foxes have been called 'Jackals of the ice', and in much of the Arctic their survival is based on scavenging from kills made by Polar Bears. In the intense coat of the ice-lands the seasonally white fox does not just keep out the coat by a full fluffed coat, but also by having hollow hairs containing air spaces that provide much needed additional insulation.

The Coyote of North America has a flexible relationship between range pattern of use and prey size. Classically it is thought of as a solitary animal, which it is in areas of small prey, but where larger prey is more abundant, Coyotes may form a small pack for hunting.

Although solitary Jackals can be found, they are usually in male-female pairs, which are more successful at hunting. From a detailed study in the Serengeti it was found that not only did some young jackals not leave their parents for a year, but that this occurred for the majority of pairs. They remained as non-breeding 'helpers', and although this was often just one animal, as more remained so the survival rate of the current year's pups improved.

The Ethiopian Wolf used to be called the Simien Jackal; this upland-living canid's available prey is small, consequently it hunts alone but returns to family groups, and again has a system of a breeding pair with non-breeding 'helpers' that regurgitate food for the pups.

Another member of the dog family sharing the name 'wolf' is the Maned Wolf of the grasslands of South America, from its looks often described as a 'long-legged fox' or a 'fox on stilts'. Although this is a large and distinctive animal, it is an endangered one, and as with some of the smaller canids, we do not know enough about its life to be sure of safeguarding it. However, it is known that not only does it feed on small prey, like many canids it consumes a significant quantity of seasonally available fruit.

Juliet Clutton-Brock of London's Natural History Museum speculates that associations were formed between early people and numerous canids towards the end of the Ice Age; during this time taming occurred not just of wolves, but of Jackals, Dholes, various fox species, Bush Dogs and possibly even African Wild Dogs. She believes that the more solitary and less pack-based canids wandered off to find mates as they grew into adulthood.

Silver-backed Jackal Canis mesomelas

Arctic Fox Alopex lagopus

Hunter or scavenger?

The jackal, such as the Black-backed Jackal above, is so associated with scavenging carcasses that the Egyptians made it Anubis, god of death. Yet in the Serengeti scavenging is under 6 per cent of its diet, most of which is fruit and caught rodents.

Basenji: and the early Pharaohs

The Basenji stands out as the most distinctive of all the historic breeds. It seems probable that the dog of today would have been recognized immediately by the ancient Egyptians, and images remarkably similar to this dog have been identified on wall reliefs showing life in the early 5th Dynasty, nearly 4,500 years ago. The only apparent difference to the modern Basenji is that they are drawn with proportionately longer legs (see page 83).

Basenjis were one of a number of dogs living in ancient Egypt, and pictures show a large range, some looking like today's greyhounds, podencos and others. As the ancient Egyptian word for dogs, 'iwiw', meant 'bark', clearly the Egyptians had more than just the Basenji, as this breed's most famous feature is that the dogs do not bark.

Non-barking is just one notable feature of this ancient breed. (Although quiet, they do make other sounds, including howling.) When a Basenji really becomes alert, it develops strong frown lines on its forehead. Even its gait is different to other dogs, in that it readily trots and can keep this up for a considerable time. It still retains the upright ears of its wolf ancestor, and, like the wolf, the Basenji has only one breeding season a year.

If socialized properly Basenjis are good with people, if shy of strangers (see below). However, dominance can be an issue with other dogs.

MODERN HISTORY

▪ As a package the Basenji is clearly an ancient wilder animal than most breeds. When Egypt's might declined, it was used across northern Africa as an all-round hunting dog, using sight and scent effectively.

▪ English Victorian explorers recognized Basenjis as distinctive, and in 1895 a pair was sent to Britain, but they succumbed to distemper. In 1936 Olivia Burn, an English dog breeder, again introduced them to England, and bred them. When shown at Crufts, they caused a sensation.

Basenji

Basenji pups

In a series of classic observations by John Paul Scott and John Fuller in the USA, Basenji pups were demonstrated to become much more fearful and wary than other breeds tested, although handling when young changed that. The researchers found that Basenjis had the capacity to be more fearful and aggressive than others. They also found that Basenjis were very tolerant of other Basenjis in an enclosure than most dogs, but competed for food. Again in contrast to the other breeds compared, Basenjis were 'outstanding in their vigorous resistance to the restraint of a collar and lead'. The conclusions were that if socialized to people at an early age, the pups were tameable.

5 The origins of dogs from their DNA

Archaeology has given information on the dog's origins, understandably in fragmentary form, for some materials survive but others do not. The picture has been fleshed out by sourcing information on dogs' pasts by looking at the genetic inheritance in the DNA of dogs today.

DNA is the long double-helix molecule that carries the code to make an individual in its unique sequence of component nucleotides (or bases). There are only four base types, but the information is in their sequence. In recent years it has become possible to investigate the genetic history of a species by what has become known as molecular systematics by determining this sequence of bases for a particular section of a chosen chromosome.

In 1997 Carles Vilà and his colleagues published their findings of using this approach on mitochondrial DNA of 140 dogs (from 67 pure breeds and 5 cross-breeds), comparing this to that of wolves of 27 distinct populations, and to that of coyotes and jackals. Their data showed that the domestic dog is closer to the wolf than to the coyote or jackal, but the date did not suggest a single origin, but rather that there was continuing hybridization between wolves and dogs long after the early domestication.

While the first archaeological evidence for a distinctly domestic dog around human remains dates from about 14,000 years ago, Vilà proposed from analysis of data that the earliest point of the domestication of dogs may have occurred as early as 160,000–130,000 years ago. Such a date would have profound implications for our understanding of the dog-human relationship. The analysis also revealed that our traditional dog breeds came together from a number of individuals of different descent.

In 2002, Peter Savolainen, who had been part of the 1997 team, headed a team that extended the search to include eastern Asia, using samples from over 650 dogs. The vast majority fitted into one of three origin groups, but the one with most diversity, and therefore most likely to be the oldest, was in east Asia. While the earliest archaeological evidence is from the Middle East and Germany, this new molecular evidence clearly suggested a Far Eastern origin for the dog. From the new data Savolainen's team refined the early domestication date to 15,000–40,000 years ago, the former figure most closely matching the existing archaeological record.

Confused by the different time frames? Well, even though these new techniques are undoubtedly powerful, they are just as dependent on interpretation as is archaeology. The dependence only on excavation evidence placed the origin of the dog in the Middle East, but this overlooked the relative lack of archaeological work in China over the last 50 years. The new genetic evidence available anticipates that archaeological searches may well be equally rewarded in the Far East.

Grey Wolf

Dogs and wildlife

Although it is accepted that climate changes caused changes in conditions for wildlife, dogs may also have contributed: for example, in America the native horse is thought to have been eradicated by 12,000 years ago, and it may be that mankind was more able to carry this out if aided by the dog as a hunting companion and helper.

BREEDS CLUSTERED BY DNA SIMILARITIES

(Heidi Parker and Colleagues, 2004)

KEY

Yellow = Wolves and dogs most closely related to wolves (also known as 'ancient' breeds)

Red = 'Hunting' Group

Green = 'Herding' Group

Blue = 'Guarding' Group

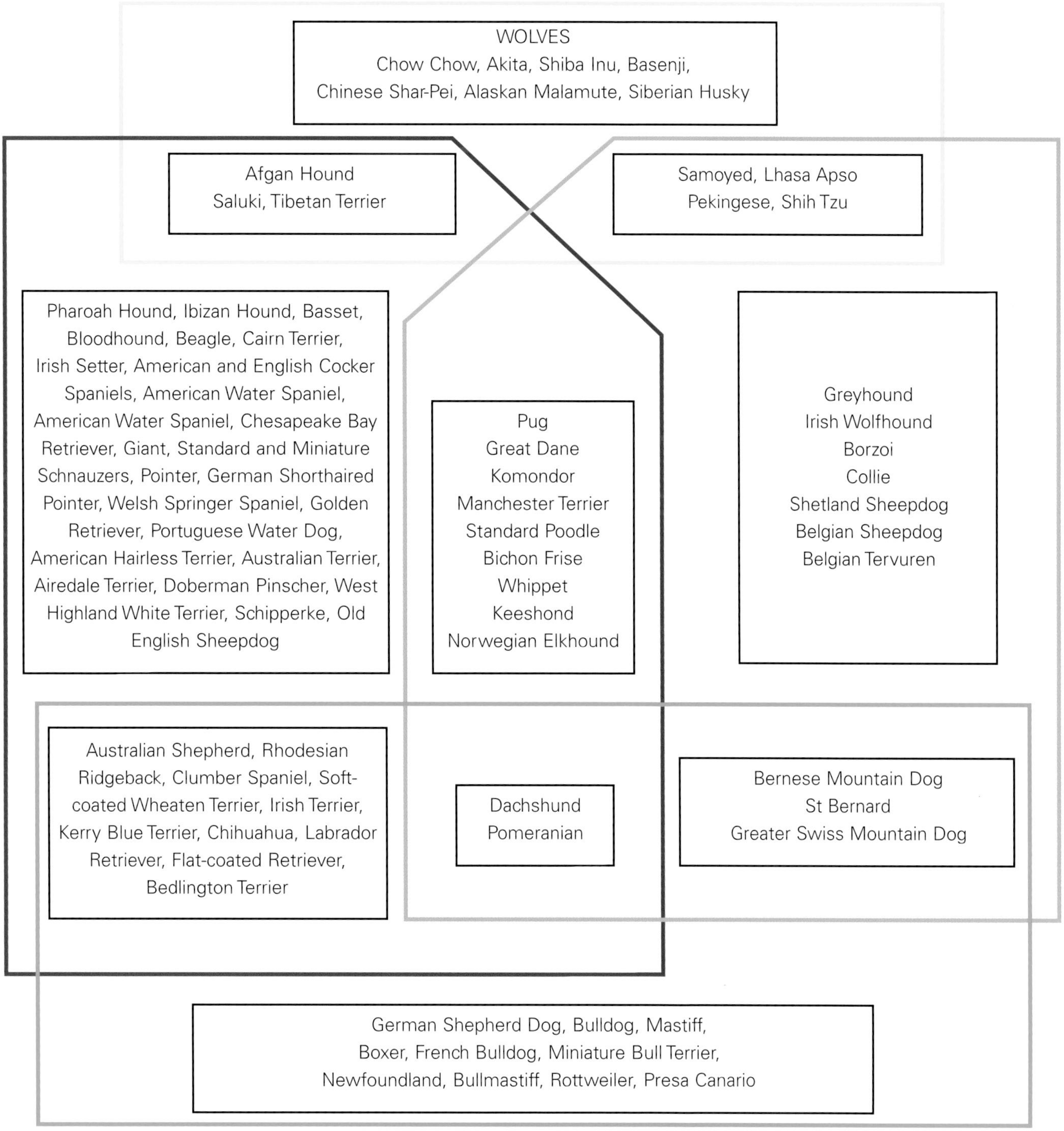

WOLVES
Chow Chow, Akita, Shiba Inu, Basenji,
Chinese Shar-Pei, Alaskan Malamute, Siberian Husky

Afgan Hound
Saluki, Tibetan Terrier

Samoyed, Lhasa Apso
Pekingese, Shih Tzu

Pharoah Hound, Ibizan Hound, Basset, Bloodhound, Beagle, Cairn Terrier, Irish Setter, American and English Cocker Spaniels, American Water Spaniel, American Water Spaniel, Chesapeake Bay Retriever, Giant, Standard and Miniature Schnauzers, Pointer, German Shorthaired Pointer, Welsh Springer Spaniel, Golden Retriever, Portuguese Water Dog, American Hairless Terrier, Australian Terrier, Airedale Terrier, Doberman Pinscher, West Highland White Terrier, Schipperke, Old English Sheepdog

Pug
Great Dane
Komondor
Manchester Terrier
Standard Poodle
Bichon Frise
Whippet
Keeshond
Norwegian Elkhound

Greyhound
Irish Wolfhound
Borzoi
Collie
Shetland Sheepdog
Belgian Sheepdog
Belgian Tervuren

Australian Shepherd, Rhodesian Ridgeback, Clumber Spaniel, Soft-coated Wheaten Terrier, Irish Terrier, Kerry Blue Terrier, Chihuahua, Labrador Retriever, Flat-coated Retriever, Bedlington Terrier

Dachshund
Pomeranian

Bernese Mountain Dog
St Bernard
Greater Swiss Mountain Dog

German Shepherd Dog, Bulldog, Mastiff,
Boxer, French Bulldog, Miniature Bull Terrier,
Newfoundland, Bullmastiff, Rottweiler, Presa Canario

6 Phoenician dogs:living fossils

The Phoenicians were the first of the great exploring maritime trading peoples. Originally they lived around the early cities of Tyre and Sidon in the Middle East, where they traded with Old Kingdom Egypt around 2500BC. By 1000BC they had settled on the coast of Cyprus, and around 750BC they founded Carthage on the north-western coast of Africa. As they spread round the Mediterranean with their settlements they took dogs, of a sort, with pricked ears, with which the Pharaohs were familiar.

Pharaoh Hound

What is so remarkable is that where the Phoenicians settled on islands, the distinctive dogs that they took with them can still be found there today as 'living fossils', recording the Phoenician spread. These ancient dogs from the Mediterranean and the Canaries are noted to have few health problems and a life span of 12 years or more.

The best known of these dogs is the Pharaoh Hound of Malta and Gozo, where they were used for centuries to catch rabbits. In 1968 a visitor from England took some of these dogs home, and felt they needed a more distinguished name than 'rabbit dog': the similarity of the dogs to those on ancient Egyptian wall paintings clinched the new name.

On Sicily, the Sicilian Hound (Cirneco dell'Etna) is an identical-looking, if slightly smaller version that was used to hunt rabbits; and a slightly heavier-looking, but otherwise identical dog, the Ibizan or Balearic Hound, or Ibizan Podenco, is a relic of the Phoenician occupation of the Balearic Islands. This was spotted by a Spanish dog breeder in the 1950s, who bred it and introduced it to a wider world. It too had a history of being used to seek and chase rabbits. Spain has an Andalusian Podenco, an echo of its Phoenician period.

Europeans seem not to have reached the Canary Islands, off the north-western Atlantic coast of Africa, until the 14th century, but the Podencos of the Canary Islands (*Podenco Canaris*), are evidence of a far earlier arrival by the Phoenicians of Carthage in the first millennium BC. On the more north-easterly of the islands, Lanzarote, the volcanic origin of the islands is starkly apparent, and in its rural communities, who have long struggled to earn a living in its hillsides of volcanic ash, the Lanzarote Podenco (top) was essential to stop rabbits destroying any crops. The dogs, which have the same lithe elegance of the other Phoenician-spread dogs, are still kept by farmers, but have succeeded as pest controllers, as rabbits are now very scarce!

The Phoenician distributed dogs, the Assyrian Mastiffs and Greyhounds are all early Middle Eastern dogs, distinct from the earlier Far East emergents suggested by the DNA findings.

Island names

The importance of the historic dogs to the islands has been claimed to reside in the Canary Islands' name, which may derive from the Latin 'canus'. For us today, the tight similarity between these groups of well separated islands' dogs is not just a map of the spread of an ancient people, but it also enables us to look with some certainty directly at the dogs of ancient Egypt and Phoenicia.

Eastern origins

7

Our best understanding of our dog's emergence and family ties comes from interpreting a combined approach of DNA analysis, archaeology, historic references and other sources. Work on the dog genome has been progressing fast; could it tell us more about gaps in our knowledge on the origins and relationships of the breeds?

In 2004 the first high-quality sequence was put into the scientific public domain by a team based in Seattle, Washington. They examined mitochondrial DNA from 85 dog breeds by taking cheek swabs from five dogs of each breed with help for sourcing from the American Kennel Club, and then looked at 96 locations on the dog genome.

They found they could place the dogs into four main clusters: three of these were relatable to function – guarding, herding and hunting – but the fourth group was one into which wolves from China, the Middle East, Europe and North America also fitted (see chart, page 17).

This fourth group of dogs contained at its core Spitz-type dogs, with a wolf-shaped head and a tail with a tendency to curl. Geographically central are two of the most distinctive of any breeds, China's Chow Chow (top) and Shar Pei. Despite its solidity, the Chow is clearly a Spitz, sometimes called the 'Chinese Spitz'. The two breeds share a famous unusual feature – a blue-black tongue.

The small Eastern breeds

In the first cluster of Wolves and Ancient Dogs (yellow in the illustration on page 17) are a group of dogs that are one removed in a mid-position from the Herding group: Pekingese and related Lhasa Apsos and Shih Tzus. Pekingese, the Little Lion Dogs, were restricted to exclusive ownership by Chinese royalty and nobility for thousands of years, and were only removed at the British sacking of Peking in 1860.

But if these royal toy companion dogs are so historic and genetically close to the wolf, how can they be among the most changed of dogs? In reality only two events needed to occur. To obtain the flatter face the rates of development of parts of the skull of the pup's head have to happen at different times to each other. Most pups are born with similar-shaped heads, but by five months the main shaping has taken place and the adult Peke face is there. Most pups of different breeds are not dissimilar in size, but the big size growth

differences occur after three months, and if this occurs at a slower rate a smaller dog occurs. Selection for novelty of such aberrant events that happen normally (but rarely) keeps alive a potential breed that natural selection is very unlikely to have favoured.

The clusters are not time maps, they are maps of similarity of DNA sequences. It is not just time that changes this: hybridizing with wolves or ancient-lineage feral or village dogs will slant the figures, making a breed seem older, while later crosses with different cluster dogs, as has taken place across history, especially to existing breeds in the 19th and 20th centuries, will make changes in another direction.

Pekingese

8 The wolf pack

The Grey Wolf ranges widely across the Northern Hemisphere, and although we associate wolves with the northern part of North America, they range across much of Asia, the Middle East and parts of Europe, occurring in up to 32 subspecies.

Although wolves are eclectic in their diet, the typical prey of northern wolves in North America is caribou and moose, and as these are a number of times heavier than an individual wolf, a pack is required to overcome them. Similarly, both the pack formation and the method of running down prey are made possible by open or relatively open habitats.

Individual packs claim an area for their use in part by howling as a pack, a chilling and evocative sound that can be heard 5–6 miles away. As individual pack territories can easily be double that across, adjacent packs are more likely to hear them if they are near the edges.

Wolves do not constantly howl – quite the reverse: howling is a very controlled activity. The pack may howl just a couple of times a day, and if a neighbouring group howls this does not mean that a pack will respond, for doing so can leave them open to another group that locates them by their call. However, if the pack has young or a fresh kill they are far more likely to be assertive and howl in response to declare ownership unambiguously. Howling carries potential risk and is more likely to be made with the greater confidence given by greater numbers in a pack. The pack size itself depends on the abundance and size of the prey.

The pack's territory is demarcated by the density of urine scent marks made by dominant males every few minutes. Towards the periphery of their ranges in the overlapping zone the scent marks of the wolves of the adjacent group trigger a hormone rush and the need to assert themselves.

The success of a wolf pack is its focus of the alpha male and female, who are normally the only ones to breed. The breeding season runs from January to April, and the dominant female normally gives birth to 4–7 pups, who usually stay out of sight underground for a month, during which time they are suckled. Once they can be fed on regurgitated food they emerge and receive food from both their parents and other wolves, 'helpers', who furnish food to ensure that the pups are large enough to travel with the pack when they are 3–5 months old.

It is the genetic readiness of the non-alpha pair animals in a pack to accept the role of being loyal supporters, for the benefit of the whole pack, that allows the dog to fit so well into our lives. However, when a non-alpha animal recognizes that its status is elevated in the pack – usually due to injury, age, weakness or death of the alpha animal – it is ready to transform itself into that very different role. This is the simple reason why in so many homes the human-dog relationship is far from ideal, and why so many dogs are euthanazed: when we abdicate the alpha role, the dog is ready to fill it.

Pack behaviour

In our relationship with our dog, so much depends on the dynamic of our small pack and our relative positions within it, that it is important if we are to understand it properly to realize where it has come from to understand 'the wolf that walks beside us'.

In the ancestor wolf and the modern dog, there is more attachment to group or pack than territory; consequently, an essential prerequisite of pack life for a group carnivore is not just dominance behaviour but also submissive behaviour. It is in this latter that dog behaviour is most profoundly different to the solitary hunting cat, which has little submissive behaviour.

Wolf packs have been found to range over 150–500 square miles, depending on the terrain and the number in the pack. Packs normally are a family group and not often more than 10–12 animals (but can be 2–22). The range is more restricted in the summer when they stay closer to the dens until the cubs are big enough to move with the pack.

We do not have to rely entirely on hindsight back to the wolf to see pack behaviour, for across countries packs of hounds have been run together to chase game. Between hunts they live a communal life in kennels. They generally score less for competitive behaviour than non-group kept breeds.

The hunting of animals with dogs was made illegal in Britain in February 2005, and officially ended a centuries-old country activity. Although the activities banned included more solitary hunting, such as hare coursing, the most recognizable image is of a pack of Foxhounds.

Foxhunting started in England in the 13th century, but the development of the modern Foxhound took place in the mid-18th century. (The American Foxhound was developed by George Washington, who crossed French hounds with English Foxhounds, resulting in more pendulous ears.)

Although Foxhounds are good-natured, energetic and friendly with people, their strong social nature with other Foxhounds has kept them typically a pack animal. They have an overwhelming instinct to pursue as a pack, and this kept them in the realm of the hunter. They can be headstrong, wilful and very destructive, and need very firm management.

Foxhounds

Hound packs

Before setting off, Foxhounds were calm and at ease, but would leap and call when the huntsman sounded the horn. Seeking the scent in the field they would be silent until one hound found the fox scent and then 'yipped' until it was sure, when it would 'bay' excitedly. This pulled the pack towards that hound, and the pack would all then 'give voice'. When they saw the prey, they would increase their pace in pursuit. The hounds did not act as individuals but as a pack, taking their instructions from the huntsman.

Feral dogs

There are feral dogs throughout the world, that is, dogs that were domesticated and have gone wild. In any area, urban or rural, there are owned dogs, some of which free-range some of the time, 'strays' that have recently wandered away, and 'fully' feral dogs that have been living wild for longer or were born into the feral state.

Egyptian Feral Dog

In recent years the press has moved feral dogs higher up the agenda. For example, in 2003 in the USA, the *National Geographic News* carried the headline 'US Facing Feral Dog Crisis', and there were supportive statistics to suggest feral dogs' responsibility in the deaths of livestock to $37,000,000 value. However, is the feral dog the culprit, or is it a problem of identity problems? Italy has been estimated to have 800,000 free-ranging dogs, of which it is believed only 80,000 are identifiable as 'fully' feral without human support, while the majority are a combination of stray dogs and those allowed to wander by their owners.

Feral dog packs

In the Apennines in the Abruzzo region of Italy Professor Luigi Boitani and colleagues monitored a pack of feral dogs, normally numbering nine adults. From 1984–87 this group was found to use an overall home range of 58 sq km (22 sq miles). A major source of food for the dogs was village dumps (there were three villages in the area).

Feral groups are formed from strays and are not normally much related, so their groups lack the stability of other canid packs. Feral dog groups generally have a low reproductive and pup survival rate, and so group size is largely maintained by village stray dogs becoming attracted during the breeding period; in Boitani's study 40 pups were born to the feral pack, of which only two survived to be adults. Over 90 per cent died within 120 days, most of the deaths occurring when den sites were left at about 2–3 months. The researchers concluded that the pack only survived due to the influx of free-ranging dogs, for the survival rate of the pups was too low otherwise; in other areas pup survival rates were higher.

In a linked study, David McDonald and colleague found that dogs ranging in Italian villages were in small groups of two to five, while hillside feral dogs were in groups of up to 10. These village dogs were also observed to scavenge in the village rubbish dumps.

Feral dog groups in the US, Japan and Italy have all been found to have an activity timetable around dawn and dusk.

In Italy, as in the USA, there has been considerable alarm expressed in the press about feral dogs killing livestock and wild animals. However, researchers' findings present a different picture of the dogs surviving as scavengers, not usually hunters. In Italy it has been found that cases of livestock killing have been by free-ranging pet or owned dogs and stray dogs, rather than by either feral dogs or wolves. The rural ferals may have formed wolf-like packs, but they were not co-operatively hunting but scavenging. The pack did have value in combating other dogs.

Controlling feral dogs

Rural, 'fully' feral dogs, which largely exist from an influx of village free-ranging dogs, may not be as much danger to livestock and wildlife as they seem to be at first sight . By comparison, the size of the urban problem with free-ranging dogs is caused largely by an irresponsible attitude that allows the dog to be a 'latchkey' animal. Eradication attempts against rural feral dogs often do not work, but controls on the fully free-ranging nature of village dogs, including better control and fencing at dumps, would have an impact.

In Australia wild dogs are accused of causing up to 30 per cent stock losses in some areas, and estimates attribute the total annual Australian agricultural cost to be $66,000,000. Control is by a mixture of trapping, shooting, poison baiting and the 'Dog Fence', which runs for 5,600km (3,475 miles) from south-eastern Queensland to western South Australia. New toxicants are being developed to control wild dogs in sheep production areas. The Australian situation is made more complicated and emotive, as the term 'wild dog' is used without discrimination both for feral domestic dogs and for dingoes and hybrids of both.

While controls were once simply aimed at total eradication, today more projects acknowledge the ambiguity of ownership. In the Galapagos Islands, the Animal Balance project, working with the islands' communities, sterilized over 2,000 dogs during 2004–6. In the Turks and Caicos islands, the Feral Dog Project gave free dog collars to schoolchildren to claim ownership of their and their communities' dogs ahead of pack capture in a large pen. Collared dogs were neutered at no cost to owners, while the feral and stray dogs were euthanazed. Of 370 dogs captured, 70 wore collars. The International Fund for Animal Welfare (IFAW) has programmes to sterilize stray and feral dogs in Russia, Turkey, Bali and elsewhere.

Nepalese Feral Dogs

'Latch-key' dogs

Free-ranging dogs, either feral or 'latch-key', occur in many parts of the world. Alan Beck carried out pioneering research on 'latch-key' dogs in Baltimore, USA, in the 1970s; by monitoring using photographs and surveying dog owners, he found that around 40 per cent were allowed to roam alone. Although the opportunity to form packs was limited by urban conditions, he occasionally encountered packs of up to 17 dogs, but half the dogs travelled alone, about a quarter in pairs, then 16 per cent in threes and 7 per cent in goups of four or five. These urban packs are potentially dangerous, but are temporary for the most part; in rural areas more stable packs of five or six dogs have been found.

10 Village dogs

How were dogs really domesticated? Was it by people selecting tamer wolf pups from packs that overlapped early man's hunting herds? Wolves may well have scavenged from kills, and there would have been a natural selecting system operating, whereby those less fearful of mankind would be more successful at gaining food by scavenging.

Village dogs, South Nepal & Indian Feral Dog and vultures scavenging carcasses

'Cross-breeds' or ancient dogs?

Are 'village mutts' cross-breeds, as most people persist in referring to them, as if they are spin-offs of modern breeds, or is Coppinger right in saying they should be recognized as having an ancient lineage, well pre-dating modern selective breeding, which really only goes back to the 18th century? Certainly today's breeds revert by outbreeding, and in many locations today's ancient village dogs are mixing with selected breeds.

I have never been a believer in man setting out to domesticate species in ancient times. In my book *The Wild Life of the Domestic Cat*, I suggested that domestic living cats emerged with exploitation of wastes around early towns that developed from agricultural surpluses: 'As with most stories of domestication man's hand was only partly responsible and if we were looking from outside of ourselves as we do at other species, we would not think in terms of "domestication", for we would see a relationship of benefit to both partners, a symbiotic dependence.'

Raymond Coppinger, the American dog biologist, has proposed that effectively the same mechanism enabled the transition from wolf into domestic dog in the earlier appearance of villages in Mesolithic times. He argues that across the world today, village dogs wander alone and scavenge from village waste dumps, and that they have remarkable similarities: under 13.5kg (30lb), 43–46cm (17–18in) high, with smooth, short coats and upright ears tipped over at the top. These dogs live around people, rather than as pets. I claimed that 'the best-bred cat is the moggie, the street cat, the farm cat – the every cat.' Coppinger has made the same claim for the village dog, the historic 'mutt'.

There is a timing concern: did villages appear early enough to be the domestication key? The believed time of the big agricultural revolution was 10,000 years ago, when villages with waste appeared, and early signs of dogs are estimated at 14,000 years ago. As hunters, people made settlements earlier, but these were generally of a more transitory nature. Hunting plains with lush, short grass were made with fire, attracting grazers (the first domestic sheep appeared 11,000 years ago), which allowed longer hunter settlement. This may have been a phase of development of greater overlap between wolf and man, with scavengeable opportunities at the site of abandoned carcasses of grazing animals. The selection for less wary proto-dogs would have occurred at these early 'waste dumps'. I have monitored and photographed feral and village dogs in many different parts of the world, and in each there is an element of seeing a re-creation of the origin of the domestic dog.

Communication

Dog communication is inherited from the wolf, but it has been modified through living with us, especially in breeds with significant body changes from their ancestors. Basic postures, tail and ear positions and movements are innate in the body form and potential behaviour, and are mediated via development and social play in the litter.

Black Labrador x Springer Spaniel & Aberdeenshire Terriers

We can easily focus on noticeable signs of body language, such as barking and tail wagging, which are clearly important, but less obvious activities and position are just as important in communication.

Like wolves, dogs spend a lot of time resting, but dogs that live with people generally spend a lot more time doing so as they don't have to hunt or scavenge for food, and are confined in their movements by walls and doors. So while your dog is quiet, start reading his mood.

Dogs that are lying down on their haunches with front legs out in front, even if a bit slumped, are very different from a dog lying on his side snoozing. The first dog is alert to the slightest encouragement to become involved, and the other is more switched off, as can be demonstrated if you give the slightest encouragement, such as walking past. The first will follow or engage within a moment, while the snoozer will require more time.

Meeting and greeting

The initial contact of unfamiliar dogs is to stand defensively, with noses together, and sniff. Female dogs focus on the head, but males usually pass on to sniff at the rear of the other dog.

WILD ORIGINS

Wild canids are kept together in packs by a bonding of wagging tails, whining and licking each other in the manner of young when their parent or feeding 'helper' returns with food. This behaviour is especially noticeable in African Wild Dogs, who have an elaborate ritualized greeting around midday. In their original context, such moves assist the food provider to regurgitate for the pups.

While the dominant male in a wolf pack may fight challengers to his position, and females may fight (often more aggressively than the males) to gain the position of the sole breeding dominant female, once relative ranks are established, these are peaceably recognized at meetings. The dominant male keeps his ears upright, while the more submissive animal shows his lower rank by flattening his ears back and keeping his tail lower than that of the dominant animal. The lower-rank wolf approaches the muzzle of the dominant wolf to the side.

If a dominant wolf grabs a lower-rank wolf with his jaws in a mouthing manner, the latter will show acceptance and submission by not retaliating and putting on a submissive 'grin'. 'Mouthing' can also be done in an appeasing way, echoing a pup's request for regurgitated food.

12

The language of dogs

Dogs have a whole body language that involves posture, tail signals and clear facial signals. However, the wide range of changes that we have made by breeding and selection has made it more difficult for dogs to have a clear indication of intent compared to their ancestors: floppy ears and long hair prevent the display of raised hackles or even seeing eyes to determine eye contact, and as a result smell and sound may have become more important.

When dogs (or wolves, as below) meet and greet, sniffing the rear end of the other dog is an important part of communication, as they gain information on the other animal's sexual status and identity. It is for this same reason that dogs often sniff at the genital area of human visitors.

In living with us dogs play a second role to our pack leader position, often with puppy-like postures. Such puppy behaviour is more exaggerated in their relationship with us (known as neotenous behaviour), and owners are often greeted by an invitation to play by their adult dogs, with erect hind legs but head and shoulders down, tail wagging and an enticing small bark.

Border Collie & Grey Wolves

SOUND LANGUAGE

Dogs have an extensive vocal vocabulary of growing and snarling, whining and howling, in addition to the characteristic bark. Barking is not just alarm and threat sounds; it is also sounded quite differently in greeting and in play and attention-seeking.

- Barking acts as a distant counter-threat to an approaching intruder. The regular repeat barking continues as long as the dog believes there to be a potential risk, but often with short re-evaluation gaps. If the intruder continues to approach, the nature of the barking changes, becoming more aggressive and more manic, and being interspersed with snarls and attack moves.

- Alarm barking is commonly picked up by other dogs a few households away and induces an alertness and readiness as well as a desire to join in, as can be seen in a group of foxhounds or kennelled dogs.

- Growling conveys important information: deep growling is a clear threat, but growling at a higher frequency shows that the dog is less confident. If it becomes whining, this is likely to convey submissive intent, the reverse of the dominant threat growl; therefore when needing to firmly control your dog, use a lower tone of voice to convey authority. Whimpering also occurs in submission, and also when a dog is in pain.

- Understandably the sounds produced by a large dog are recognizably different to those produced by small dogs, whose barking is often referred to as 'yapping'. Other dogs have this information available to them when assessing threat barking.

- Wolves howl to make contact with each other, and when dogs howl it is usually when they are alone and in need of such contact, both canine and human. At such times it has been said over the centuries that dogs are 'howling at the moon'.

Reading body language

A properly functioning relationship with a dog depends on him recognizing us as more dominant, and his therefore slotting into a submissive co-operation. Factors such as our size normally mean that most dogs happily play this role and gain confidence from its security – however, this depends on their reading clear signals from us.

In general, easy, fluid movements show a calm, relaxed dog, while stiff, jerky moves come from an ill-at-ease or aggressive dog. If your dog is feeling unwell or depressed, then he may appear less lively, with his head not held up in the usual way, and he may be less interested in food.

As the wolf's life depended on the pack, the pack mentality is innate within the dog. Unrestrained aggression could only occur if the survival of the individual was not dependent on the success of the pack, so this must be tempered and is achieved by the counterbalance of submissive behaviour.

A submissive dog may go towards a more dominant animal with its body and head low, shoulders rocking, and the tail low and wagging vigorously, and lick or nuzzle around the face of the dominant animal. This is an echo of pups approaching their mother. Owners are often greeted in a similar way by their dogs.

As a dog lowers his profile he is showing a submissive, less aggressive stance: the extreme of this is to go low to the ground and roll over to expose his underbelly to potential attack; sometimes he will urinate. In general, at a meeting of two dogs the more aggressive one will try to look taller and larger, raising his hackles, while a dog that lowers his position and licks his lips is being submissive.

THE TAIL

- The wagging tail for owners is synonymous with a happy dog, and when you arrive home the dog will 'flag up' that he is pleased to see you.

- Your dog's tail held in a neutral mid-position when wagging with a relaxed stance shows a dog wanting friendly interaction. However, the wag is not just about pleasure; it is primarily excitement, and a fast and forceful wagging, rigid upright tail is likely to be aggressive.

- Again, the wagging may be slower and more definite, also conveying aggressive intent; certainly if tail wagging is combined with raising the hackles or piloerection of the shoulder hair, then beware.

- A tail wagged low shows a submissive or fearful position, and may be combined with other submissive behaviour.

Reading signs

Understanding signals is helpful to owners' interpretation of their dog's moods and reactions. These two 'teenager' pups (right) are meeting, and the spaniel is standing upright, leaning slightly forward with a raised tail and a definite stare which intimidates the young terrier who shows concern by his pulled back ears, wide eyes and by leaning back. They were just assessing each other; no fight ensued.

Jack Russell Terrier & Springer Spaniel

14 Reading facial expressions

Owners who have a good long-term relationship with their dogs often say that they see absolute trust on looking into their dogs' eyes. However, if you are with a dominant dog with whom you have not established a good relationship, beware giving an intense stare, as this can provoke aggressive action.

A dominant dog will stare down a more submissive dog, who will look away; sheepdogs will adopt a similar unblinking fixed eye, much in the way seen in wolves or hunting dogs towards their prey, and from which sheep will shy away. A frightened dog looks about wide-eyed, with perceptively enlarged pupils and whites of the eyes often more apparent.

A dominant dog asserting its position over another will project its head forwards, whilst an intimidated dog will do the reverse. When a dominant dog bares its teeth, the lips are drawn back, exposing the teeth more fully to the extent that not only are the big canines visible but the front row of incisors are seen clearly, while the dog also snarls.

However, such clarity of signalling often averts a fight, as the less dominant dog will attempt to make itself less of a threat by backing away; it can also similarly sort out the 'huff and puff' competition between dogs in a household. When made by a possessive dominant dog towards its owner over a chair or the dog's food bowl, this behaviour can be intimidating. However, not all facial expressions are about aggression and submission, and when a dog is relaxed so will be its facial muscles.

The position of a dog's ears are also important in reading a dog's intent – this aspect is thus very hard to recognize in dogs with heavy, floppy ears, such as Basset Hounds or Spaniels. When your dog is paying alert attention to you, his ears are erect (or as erect as the breed can manage), and when a challenge between two dogs is under way, the higher ranking one will have his erect ears pointing forwards while the more submissive animal will have his ears flat and back. This subdued ear position is also seen when dogs are being reprimanded.

For the dog's wild ancestors, clear and unambiguous signals were critical for survival, during a hunt or when sorting out rank. However, while the intentions of a Norwegian Buhund (top) can be read easily by other dogs, the heavy jowls and skin folds around the eyes of a Basset (above right) can make expressions hard to interpret.

Basset Hound

SAFETY FIRST

New research shows that children under four years old are less good at interpreting dog behaviour than older children, as they focus on the face rather than the whole animal: they may see a fearful dog as being a happy one, and risk fear-biting.

What is a 'safe' face?

- *Neutral*: relaxed face
- *Greeting familiar human*: ears relaxed, mouth relaxed open, 'greeting grin' (friendly submission = our smile)

What is a 'risky' face?

- *Alert threat*: ears erect, eyes staring, nose wrinkles, teeth bared, tail and hackles up (don't advance, may attack)
- *Submissive*: ears back, eyes diverted, licks lips, head down (body and tail lowered)
- *Ambivalent submission*: like submissive but head more up, eyes staring, tensed 'mimic grin' of bared teeth (may fear-bite)

Scent marking

Scent marking is important to dogs for information about other dogs in the area. Dogs raise or cock their leg to urinate against trees, and also try to 'overwrite' the scent message of another dog's droppings by defecating on or next to it. Inspection of one dog by another similarly involves sniffing urino-genital areas to determine the identity and sexual status of the other animal.

Urine marking is mainly a male prerogative, and when householders have problems with their dog's marking it is normally with dominant male dogs with high testosterone levels. However, we need to recognize that the dog has a strong urge to mark its territorial area. (Females can occasionally urine mark like a male, but not normally against lamp-posts or other upright fixtures.)

For us to understand territory, the normal definition, which applies to territorial animals such as cats, is the area they will defend; in comparison, the home range is the area that the animal lives in. However, the relative mobility of the ancestral pack gave dogs a higher attachment to pack protection than absolute territory.

Dogs will strongly defend the area of their use in our houses and gardens, particularly at key arousal points such as doors, gates and fences. They may have a perception of a mutual care area within which their pack should have the confidence of ownership. However, due to the mobility of their ancestral packs and our current 'pack', our dogs tend to defend and mark wherever they are.

Urine marking is not limited to the immediate area, for a regular walk is punctuated with regular urine marking by dominant males. Marking urination can be told apart from 'normal' urination, as the volume dispatched in the former is much smaller, and normally follows a lot of sniffing about, checking out other scent marks.

Having marked, the dog may go through a ritualized scraping of the ground using both back and front paws. Normally the dog does not scratch the area he has just marked, but immediately adjacent, forming a visual signal that draws attention to his scent mark.

The act of marking is an assertion of dominance and ownership, and consequently it is often carried out directly on to existing scenting spots of other dogs. When a new dog comes on to the block and leaves a scent, resident dogs will mark more often to re-establish territorial ownership.

Marking function should not be visualized as having a territorial boundary, for marking is undertaken more widely across the claimed area, and the dog's own scent gives confidence of his right to be there. At the same time, reading others' scent marks not only gives evidence of who else is about, but these other scents are a challenge to a dominant dog and provide him with useful information, not least about the sexual status of female dogs.

Before male dogs become sexually mature, marking lacks significance; they start marking at puberty.

Unusual postures

Dogs are inventive in their range of urinating positions, which range from the classic male cocking his leg against a tree or lamp-post, and squatting, to positively gymnastic moves of reversing up against a vertical object and taking the weight on the front paws, effectively doing a handstand or pawstand.
As if this were not adventurous enough, sometimes it is developed into variants such as standing on the front legs, going into a squat and then lifting one hind leg.

British Bulldog

Shiba Inu &
Samoyed

Pekingese &
Cavalier
King Charles
Spaniel

2

Breeds

Dalmatian

Selecting the breed for the job

Arising from the early lines of heavy, round-headed mastiff types and sleek sighthounds, further variety appeared over time. In addition, geographical conditions selectively allowed survival of types of dogs to match the local climate, with thick coats for the cold. Different historic breed types thus began to appear through a combination of natural and artificial selection, and the shaping and selection of dogs for differing functional roles, like the Hovawart (left).

Many old breeds had a similarity to present-day forms as early as the 18th and 19th centuries. Then, as people moved more to the cities, with urbanization came mechanization and industrialization, and man and dog power were less called upon to work in the field. However, the growth of the suburbs and the increase of leisure time gave an audience for the new dog shows, and led to a formalization of breeds.

Although the breeds were then allocated groups, these are not universal. The classification systems by the UK's Kennel Club (KC) in 1873 and the American Kennel Club (AKC) in 1884 were made in a time when dogs were still working, and thus reflect the jobs the breeds fulfilled. They agree in most cases, but not entirely: for instance, to the AKC the Bichon Frise and the Löwchen are Non-Sporting dogs, while to the KC they are Toys. The group classifications in the following pages are the ones with which most people are familiar, and are a balance between the KC and AKC's breed recognitions.

Kennel Club: Hounds, Gundogs, Terriers, Working, Pastoral, Utility, Toy

American Kennel Club: Hounds, Sporting, Terriers, Working, Herding, Non-Sporting, Toy

BEYOND 'BREEDS'

With a wide range of types of breeds, no group classification system is going to hold all breeds neatly.

To start with, there have been far more breeds identified than registered – Desmond Morris investigated over 1,000 breeds. Some breeds fit into more than one group of most registration organisation classifications: for example, the Poodle is placed in the Utility group by the KC, and the equivalent Non-Sporting group by the AKC. However, its history is that of a hard-working water retriever – even its name derives from the Low German 'puddeln', meaning 'to splash in water' – and its later fashion role was the catalyst for the change of grouping (see also page 141).

Alternative groupings

In 1755 Buffon grouped dogs by ear shapes, and Cuvier used skull shapes in the 19th century. Classifications have also been made on appearance, such as the apparently related Spitz group (Japanese Spitz, right). Now a new form of grouping is emerging, DNA clusters of dogs (see page 17); there are some similarities to KC/AKC groups but also differences.

Japanese Spitz

Breed behaviour

The behaviour characteristics of dog breeds have been accentuated by build selection. For example, herding dogs have inhibited chase and attack moves by deference to the shepherd; pursuit hounds are either primarily dependent on sight (such as Borzois and Greyhounds) or on scent (such as Bloodhounds); and historically, guard and attack dogs were selected for size, like the flock guarding Kuvasz (right).

In a series of behaviour tests, hunting breeds (Beagles, Basenjis, Cocker Spaniels and Terriers) scored higher in tests involving working things out independently for food rewards, while Shetland Sheepdogs, who have been selected to perform complex tasks under instruction from their shepherd masters, did poorly.

Breed differences in behaviour can be seen during training, so do not expect all breeds to behave the same. Basenjis initially fight vigorously against a leash, but settle down to accept it after some ten days, and although they do not bark, they will complain by howls. Shetland Sheepdogs also don't take to a leash readily, but snake around their owner's legs in early training. By contrast, Spaniels, Beagles and Terriers readily take to wearing a leash.

In general breed comparison tests, Cocker Spaniels were found to be easy to train overall, while Basenjis and Beagles can be hard work to train; between the two extremes, Shetland Sheepdogs and Wire-haired Fox Terriers score well at some tasks and badly in others.

Your dog's breed and sex will largely dictate many of his distinctive characteristics. However, all dogs are individuals, and your dog's personality, just as with people, depends a lot upon past experiences, particularly in early life. Whether or not a pup was properly socialized has a profound influence on interaction later in life. Your dog may be dominant or submissive, confident or insecure, co-operative or unco-operative – most dogs are a mix of all these.

There are definite breed differences that are genetically inherited in behavioural potential just as much as in the body appearance. Although centuries of selection to certain types of dog occurred, the formalization to standardized breeds only became more absolute in the latter part of the 19th century with the advent of the show bench. The implications are not just for the origins of the dog, but also for how we choose to select when breeding. Breeds that formerly were bred for aggression can be made more tractable by actively being selected for a gentler, tamer disposition (see page 71).

PUP-LIKE ADULTS

Some fully grown dogs retain the 'adult' wolf-like features of a pointed face, but others, such as the Pyrenean Mountain Dog, have floppy ears and rounded, puppy-shaped faces.

This livestock guardian has little predatory behaviour. In contrast, pointed-faced Greyhounds, and other sight-hounds with strong predatory behaviour, attack prey on sight. Midway, gundogs such as Spaniels hunt, but are inhibited from making the kill. Virtually all dog and wolf pups have the same round-shaped face when born, but by four months the heads are nearing adult shape (if not size). The range of adult head shapes occurs due to different rates of growth of parts of the developing skull; the rates of skull growth of a German Shepherd Dog are similar to the rates of the ancestor wolf, for example. However, in the extreme case of a rounded head, the Bulldog has very slow-growing nasal bones, and so the palate buckles up. The genes that cause this are those that affect timing in development for structure and behaviour. The word for these timing changes that give breeds their different appearance is heterochrony (Greek for 'changing time'), and slowing shape development to be more pup-like is neotony. The same is also true for limb bone development, accounting for height differences.

Cocker Spaniel (working clip)

18 Hounds

Hounds trace their origins to the early sighthounds of the Middle East, and are the earliest dogs used by mankind for hunting. The sighthounds left a dynasty of swift, sleek hounds, the Greyhound, Saluki and Afghan, while the later scenthounds exchanged speed for stamina. Packs of hunting hounds were developed in the medieval period for hunting the royal deer and, centuries later, the fox. If you have a hound as a pet, be aware that after so many centuries of hunting lineage, the hunter remains within.

Basenji

Size:
Male
43cm (17in)
11kg (24lb)

Female
40cm (16in)
9.5kg (21lb)

This most ancient hunting breed is famed for not barking; however, it is not silent, as it makes a 'yodelling' noise when it becomes excited.

Temperament: The ancient Basenji can seem very independent and aloof, especially with strangers. The dogs are always alert, don't initially take to a lead and can have control problems, such as chewing things, especially when young; they will want to dominate other dogs in a home. Basenjis have lots of curiosity, and make good lively companions. They are very clean and lack a 'doggy' odour, but they meticulously clean themselves in the same way as cats.

Exercise: Likes brisk walks, but does not require more than medium amounts. Doesn't like cold and wet.

Grooming: Minimal.

Afgan Hound

Size:
Male
74cm (29in)
27kg (60lb)

Female
69cm (27in)
22.5kg (50lb)

A stunning show-stopper of a dog, its origins were as a sight-hunter to catch prey in the mountainous areas of Afghanistan. It is probably a long-haired variant of the Saluki, adapted to colder conditions.

Temperament: The Afghan has a superior, dignified manner and always appears elegant. Although affectionate, it scores highly as a dominant dog; this can show itself in ignoring an owner's requests and remaining independent, unless the owner is properly established early on as the senior partner in the relationship. Afghans tend to ignore visitors.

Exercise: Needs a lot of exercise, and loves to run.

Grooming: A considerable amount of time is needed daily to keep the stunning coat tangle-free.

Greyhound

Size:
Male
76cm (30in)
32kg (70lb)

Female
71cm (28in)
27kg (60lb)

Only the cheetah can run faster, and the Greyhound is claimed to be the oldest of breeds. This was the dog of kings, used to quickly catch prey in an explosive dash, attaining 64km/h (40mph), and has been recorded in drawings and paintings across the ages.

Temperament: Despite the athletic build, this is a gentle, affectionate animal, and track-retired Greyhounds readily take to home life. They are good natured with strangers, unless these are small animals, which they will chase and kill; they will chase and seize retreating cats. For these reasons, the choice of safe open spaces for exercise needs careful consideration.

Exercise: Needs to run, but only has medium exercise requirements, as Greyhounds are sprinters, not long-distance runners.

Grooming: Minimal.

This is an animal that needs room – it is the largest known breed. The Irish Wolfhound is famed in legend for pursuing and destroying wolves, which it helped to eradicate in Ireland by the end of the 18th century.

Temperament: These are gentle giants. They are generally friendly with family, strangers and children, although their large size can be a problem in pushing small children off balance. Although Irish Wolfhounds can be lethargic at home, be cautious, for they are large animals to control if their chase instincts are triggered on a walk.

Exercise: Enjoys a turn of speed and long rambles, but only has medium exercise needs.

Grooming: The rough coat needs regular attention.

Irish Wolfhound

Size:
Male
79cm (31in)
55kg (120lb)

Female
71cm (28in)
41kg (90lb)

Basset Hounds are not noted for their speed, but they are very thorough and determined when following a scent; being short-legged, they suited huntsmen on foot. Bassets were developed in France, but were crossed with Bloodhounds in England in the 19th century, producing a lugubrious-looking hound with remarkably long ears.

Temperament: Steady and placid, not aggressive but affectionate. However, if Bassets are set on something, they can be stubborn. They are not excitable, having low activity levels, or ready to be trained easily, but this is accompanied by a lack of destructiveness. With distinctive, sonorous voices, these are dogs with character.

Exercise: Steady.

Grooming: Not demanding.

Basset Hound

Size:
Male
38cm (15in)
23kg (50lb)

Female
33cm (13in)
20kg (44lb)

There is a long-running controversy as to which group this dog should be in – it may have a hound ancestry, but because it was selected and bred to go into the earth after badgers, its function was that of a terrier. There are different versions, but the glamour version is the long-haired type. With a long back and short legs, this dog has had a tendency to back problems.

Temperament: Dachshunds are gentle, affectionate and generally good tempered, but they are highly reactive as watchdogs to what they consider intruders, and can then be territorially defensive.

Exercise: Not demanding.

Grooming: The long-haired form needs regular grooming, as the coat can trail in mud.

Dachshund

Size:
Standard
20–25cm (8–10in)
9–12kg (20–26lb)

19 Sporting dogs and gundogs

These dogs make up a very recognizable group, whose original role was to assist in the hunting and retrieval of game; they could not be too excitable or noisy, which makes them great companions. Two of the world's most consistently popular breeds, the Labrador and the Golden Retriever, are in this group.

Irish Red & White Setter

Size:

Male
69cm (27in)
29kg (65lb)

Female
63cm (25in)
27kg (60lb)

This is the historic setter of Ireland; in the hunting field it was more popular that its cousin the Red Setter, as the white in the coat was easier to see and the dog was thus less likely to be shot accidentally. Both types are energetic setters who systematically 'quarter' about until they detect the game bird, then crouch still to allow the hunter to shoot over them.

Temperament: Its Kennel Club standard states 'happy, good natured and affectionate'. An athlete, this is an energetic and spirited dog. Training should not be too firm and can take a little longer than with other gundogs, but once trained, the dogs are regarded as reliable. The Red and White Setter is less excitable than the Red.

Exercise: Demands huge amounts of activity.

Grooming: The wonderful 'feathering' is a mud and burr magnet, so the coat needs a lot of regular attention.

Brittany Spaniel

Size:

Male
53cm (20in)
15kg (33lb)

Female
49cm (19in)
14kg (30lb)

The Brittany, or Breton Spaniel, is the smallest of the French Spaniels, whose French breed club's motto is 'Maximum quality for minimum size'. Despite its name, it is mainly a pointer retriever (due to matings with setters and pointers from England in the 19th century), and this combination enabled it to do most things in the hunting field.

Temperament: The Brittany Spaniel has an energetic and busy nature, with a desire to please, which can be seen both in the field, where it works close to its owner, and equally in the house. Although it is playful and usually fine with strangers or children, be cautious of breed lines that are not.

Exercise: Thrives on a high level of exercise, and has good stamina.

Grooming: Not demanding.

Labrador Retriever

Size:

Male
58cm (23in)
26kg (58lb)

Female
56cm (22in)
24kg (53lb)

Commonly just known as the Labrador, this is the world's most popular pedigree dog. Although it has the upmarket image of an English gentleman's gundog, it started in extreme conditions, as the Newfoundland fisherman's dog that worked in the cold Canadian sea, pulling fisherman's nets by cork floats. Taken to Britain by fishermen in the 19th century, Labrador Retrievers were welcomed as gundogs due to their 'soft mouths' not harming the game.

Temperament: Known for their reliability, Labradors are much loved as devoted family pets. Normally very good with children, they enjoy being with the family. This intelligent dog is friendly and easily trained.

Exercise: Needs vigorous and regular exercise; lack of proper exercise can lead to destruction chewing. Readily takes to water.

Grooming: The short double coat has excellent waterproof qualities, and is easy to maintain with regular brushing.

Different types of Sporting dogs were bred and trained to carry out sections of a hunt, and not just to follow the instinct to chase and catch: Pointers detect game birds and stand pointing towards them; Setters detect game birds, but crouch down under the line of fire; Spaniels flush game from cover into nets or up to the gun line of fire; Retrievers recover shot game and retrieve it.

Heights and weights are given for guidance only. Heights are taken at the withers (see pages 10–11).

These are wonderful dogs, hugely popular both as a pet and with field sportsmen. The breed was developed in the mid-19th century by Lord Tweedsmouth, officially as a mix of Wavy-coated Retriever and Tweed Water Spaniel.

Temperament: Kindly, gentle, intelligent and confident, tolerant of children and loyal, Golden Retrievers are excellent family dogs. Easily trained, they enjoy fieldwork and retain a playful nature. They score low in dominance towards owners, and do not readily show aggression to other dogs. Although fair watchdogs, they do not usually have problems of excessive barking.

Exercise: Loves being out in the field and enjoys long vigorous walks, preferably with the opportunity to go swimming.

Grooming: The coat needs daily brushing, with attention to the undercoat. The 'feathers' and tail need combing to remove mud.

Golden Retriever

Size:
Male
60cm (24in)
36kg (80lb)

Female
56cm (22in)
24kg (53lb)

A smart-looking dog, the Vizsla is the national dog of Hungary, and is sometimes called the Hungarian Pointer. Vizslas have a spectacular russet gold colour, and in Hungary have a good reputation as a pointer/retriever. Their ancestors are thought to date back to the arrival of the Magyar people in Europe over 1,000 years ago.

Temperament: A lively, yet gentle and sensitive dog, the intelligent and easily trained Vizsla responds to a gentle yet firm approach. Vizslas have very affectionate natures, but can be protective, and can be boisterous or destructive if exercised insufficiently.

Exercise: Thrives on running and walks, and enjoys swimming.

Grooming: The short, dense coat has a sheen and is easy to care for with a firm brush. The rarer long-haired type needs daily brushing.

Hungarian Vizsla

Size:
Male
64cm (25in)
30kg (66lb)

Female
60cm (24in)
25kg (55lb)

The role of the Springer was to 'spring' or flush out the birds into the air, historically for hawks and later for guns. This large spaniel is believed to be bred into most other spaniel breeds (except the Clumber); the Kennel Club standard states: 'of ancient and pure origins, oldest of sporting gundogs.'

Temperament: Friendly, happy and enthusiastic, Springer Spaniels score high for playfulness. Their biddable nature allows them to be easily trained, and they are normally patient with children. For outgoing and lively families, a Springer Spaniel normally makes a good family pet, but needs proper exercise.

Exercise: Enjoys regular vigorous exercise, and has good stamina.

Grooming: While the coat is reasonably easy to care for with brushing, the 'feathers' on the legs pick up mud readily, and the hairy ears need attention.

English Springer Spaniel

Size:
Male
48cm (19in)
18kg (40lb)

Female
46cm (18in)
16kg (35lb)

Terriers

These are known as the 'earth workers' – when the Romans invaded Britain, they found these dogs and called them 'terrarii' (from the Latin 'terra', meaning earth), and the name stuck. The majority of these very determined pest controllers originated in Britain: some went down burrows to catch their prey, while others caught burrowing animals such as rats, rabbits, foxes and badgers.

Bull Terrier

Size:
48cm (19in)
32kg (70lb)

Although classed as a Terrier, this is a designer fighting dog. In 1835 bull baiting was banned, so gamblers turned to dogfights, and this dog was created by crossing a Bulldog with a Black and Tan Terrier. When dogfights were banned, it became a show dog. In the film *Oliver*, Bill Sykes's dog, Bullseye, was a Bull Terrier.

Temperament: With its hard bite, determination and high pain threshold, this dog can be a danger to other dogs if not properly socialized to dogs when young. Bull Terriers are usually good with people and devoted to their owners, but socialization to children and other people is sensible. Be cautious with exposure to cats.

Exercise: Enjoys exercise, which needs to be regular but moderate. Due to the breed's solidity and reputation, keep a Bull Terrier on a lead in public places.

Grooming: Easy: use a damp cloth to rub dirt off the short, flat coat.

Cairn Terrier

Size:
Male
33cm (13in)
8kg (18lb)

Female
30cm (12in)
8kg (17lb)

Cairns are mounds of stones, found among the heather all over the Western Highlands of Scotland, and this small terrier would kill the rodents hiding in them. It has been claimed as the ancestral Scottish terrier, and its shaggy coat gave this small dog much-needed protection against Highland weather.

Temperament: Perky, feisty, loyal, courageous, energetic, fearless, alert and affectionate to owners, this is indeed the archetypal terrier. Cairns are excitable and likely to bark, and they can be possessive over toys and may harm cats; however, they are easily trained.

Exercise: Enjoys running about a garden, but if it doesn't have that outlet it will need to be walked.

Grooming: Although the coat is shaggy, it only needs to be brushed a few times a week.

Soft-coated Wheaten Terrier

Size:
Male
50cm (20in)
20kg (45lb)

Female
48cm (19in)
18kg (40lb)

This dog's coat really is soft. Although it is claimed to be the oldest of Irish terriers, it is now uncommon in Ireland, but is very popular in the USA. It was used to dig for foxes and badgers, but was also a general farm dog, killing rats, droving cattle and keeping watch.

Temperament: Good-tempered, friendly, lively, even exuberant, a good watchdog, intelligent and easy to train, the Soft-coated Wheaten's strong hunting instinct can be a problem with cats and other small animals. It is important to properly socialize these dogs, or there can be problems with meeting other dogs and owners may encounter dominance problems.

Exercise: Needs regular moderate to high exercise.

Grooming: It is important to begin daily grooming in puppyhood. A medium-toothed comb is helpful for preventing tangles in the single coat.

This short-legged dog, from the rugged Western Isles in Scotland, was described by John Cajus in the 16th century, when it was used to hunt foxes, badgers, weasels and otters. Famed for its hard coat and distinctive ears, the breed was popularized by Queen Victoria, and later Queen Alexandra; the coat of the modern animal is softer.

Temperament: While affectionate to owners, Skye Terriers can be aggressive to people they don't know, and at best reserved; there can also be problems in meeting other dogs. As with similar small terriers, they can be highly reactive, easily aroused and a danger to cats. The Kennel Club breed standard calls the Skye Terrier a 'one-man' dog, and owners may have dominance problems.

Exercise: Needs moderate regular exercise.

Grooming: There is a double coat, with a soft woolly one under the outer long coat. Daily coat care can be demanding.

Skye Terrier

Size:
Male
26cm (10in)
11.5kg (25lb)

Female
25cm (10in)
11kg (24lb)

This small East Anglian breed has only been around for 40 years since its first recognition in the UK. Its formation was based on only a small variation from its predecessor, the Norfolk being a drop-eared variant of the prick-eared Norwich Terrier, and the origin of both is found in the small ratting terriers of sporting undergraduates at Cambridge University in the 19th century.

Temperament: This small terrier is described in the Kennel Club breed standard as 'a demon for its size'. These fearless little dogs, however, are not only affectionate with their owners, but generally don't pick fights with other dogs and are friendly with strangers. They do chase cats, and good socialization is advisable.

Exercise: Enjoys country walks, and will probably show keen interest in holes in the ground.

Grooming: Professional attention twice a year is advised.

Norfolk Terrier

Size:
25cm (10in)
6.5kg (14lb)

Dating from the 17th century, this is one of the earliest and shortest of the Irish terrier breeds. It gained its rugged character and appearance in the Wicklow Mountains, where it was developed for badger hunting, and despite its size, it is imbued with courage. This is not a common breed, but is appreciated by its owners; unusually for a terrier, it is relatively quiet.

Temperament: Active, independent and packed full of curiosity, yet affectionate and indeed docile with owners, these dogs are game and ready to keep going, but can be highly reactive and, like most terriers, a danger to cats. They can also be aggressive to other dogs, so good socialization is necessary.

Exercise: Enjoys a medium-to-high amount of exercise.

Grooming: The harsh-textured coat does not need much grooming, and requires only medium attention.

Glen of Imaal Terrier

Size:
36cm (14in)
16kg (35lb)

21

Working dogs

The group termed 'Working dogs' traditionally used in the UK was so huge that it was subdivided into Working and Herding in the USA and some other countries and now it has also been divided in the UK into Working and Pastoral, where working dogs are hauling or pulling dogs, such as Huskies, and guarding dogs, such as Bull Mastiffs.

Bernese Mountain Dog

Size:

Male
71cm (28in)
50kg (110lb)

Female
66cm (26in)
45kg (100lb)

The handsome Swiss Mountain dog, the Berner Sennenhund, was often called the Cheesery dog, as it was primarily a haulage dog that pulled small carts of cheese and other farm products to market. It doubled as a general mountain farm dog, and also herded cattle.

Temperament: Always seeming to wear a smile, this is a cheerful, loyal, willing, confident dog who is normally excellent as a rural family dog, and is usually good with children when properly socialized. However, Berneses' loyalty can make it hard for them to change to a new owner as an adult, and you should be cautious of some breed lines, as these may have aggression problems.

Exercise: Needs regular moderate exercise.

Grooming: Brushing on a daily basis is necessary.

Bull Mastiff

Size:

Male
69cm (27in)
60kg (130lb)

Female
66cm (26in)
50kg (110b)

This impressive guard dog resulted from a 19th-century cross between the Bulldog and the Mastiff and was used as a gamekeeper's dog to pursue and overcome poachers. Because the cross was with the original Bulldogs, which had less flat faces than today, the Bull Mastiff does not have the same degree of breathing problems as the modern Bulldog.

Temperament: As watchdogs, Bull Mastiffs are second to none, but they are otherwise calm, loyal and tolerant of children, and normally don't mean to knock over the latter. However, when walking out the owner should be strong, and to avoid aggression to other dogs and strange people, the dog needs good socialization.

Exercise: Enjoys moderate exercise.

Grooming: Easy.

Siberian Husky

Size:

Male
60cm (23in)
24kg (52lb)

Female
54cm (21in)
19.5kg (43lb)

Sled dogs have the overall name of huskies, and once there were many local types. In Alaska, the Alaskan Malamute (top) was a large heavy-hauling dog, and the nearest equivalent Old World dog is the ancient breed of the Siberian Husky, which was used by the Chukchi people for lighter loads over long distances.

Temperament: These beautiful dogs were born to pull sledges in cold climates, not to live in the suburbs – when underexercised they can become destructive and dig their way out of gardens. Siberian Huskies are friendly, gentle, quiet, intelligent and not excitable; however, their thick coats make them uncomfortable in hot climates.

Exercise: Needs considerable quantities of vigorous exercise: pulling a wheeled rig is enjoyable. Avoid too much exercise in hot weather.

Grooming: The thick coat needs to be groomed a few days a week, especially when moulting.

The Boxer is near in appearance and mobility to the earlier form of the Bulldog, and the Boxer's ancestor, the Bullenbeiszer, was used in Germany for bull-baiting and boar-hunting. The first registered Boxer in 1895 resulted from a cross with a white English Bulldog.

Temperament: Boxers are loyal to the family and normally good with children, but can be boisterous. They respond well to training and are used for military and guard work. The adult male can have problems of aggression with other dogs and thus needs socializing. Boxers can become overprotective.

Exercise: Needs vigorous daily exercising and play. Young children should not walk Boxers unsupervised, due to problems with other dogs.

Grooming: This is easy, as the short, smooth coat lies flat to the body. (Watch out for slobbery drool on clothing, however.)

Boxer

Size:
Male
63cm (25in)
32kg (70lb)

Female
59cm (24in)
27kg (60lb)

A dog of superlatives: the largest, the heaviest, of ancient lineage, and the rescuer of people lost in the Swiss mountains. The breed probably originates from mastiffs that were initially used as guard dogs; by the 18th century the hospice founded by St Bernard de Menthon in 980 was using the dogs to rescue stranded travellers. They were bred to be larger in the 19th century.

Temperament: Gentle, friendly but dignified, steady, benevolent and normally tolerant of children, these intelligent dogs respond well to training. However, a dog of this size and strength is a real problem, even on a lead, if not properly trained and socialized, and some breed lines could present dominance problems.

Exercise: Needs moderate, regular exercise.

Grooming: The coat is relatively easy to groom daily with comb and brush. Pay extra attention at the twice-yearly moult.

St Bernard

Size:
Male
up to 91cm (36in)
90kg (200lb)

Female
up to 64cm (26in)
70kg (160lb)

This Hungarian breed has been described as 'not so much a dog, more a cord rug'. But don't be fooled – these are very much large dogs, and although their distinctive coat blended in with a flock of sheep, they were not there to herd but to guard, with the element of surprise on their side.

Temperament: Although devoted to their owners, Komondors have a guarding nature that shows itself in wariness towards strangers, and they can be aggressive towards both people and other dogs. The dog's facial expression cannot be seen, so its mood can be hard to judge. This is not a dog for the timid (or urban) owner.

Exercise: Needs moderate exercise.

Grooming: The coat cannot be brushed or combed; to avoid forming large matted areas, the hair is gently divided into cords. The coat all too easily picks up a large part of the countryside.

Komondor

Size:
Male
65cm (25in)
51kg (112lb)

Female
60cm (24in)
50kg (110lb)

Pastoral and herding dogs

Where there were herds of domestic stock there was usually a herding dog; many of these dogs were thickly coated to protect them against hillside weather (and possibly to blend in more with the sheep). Cattle dogs, such as Corgis, were smaller. With herding dogs the predatory action of the chase has been inhibited to the pursuit of herding.

Bearded Collie

Size:
Male
56cm (22in)
25kg (55lb)

Female
53cm (21in)
22kg (48lb)

Also known as the Highland Collie, this dog seems to have been primarily a drover's dog, bringing hillside sheep and cattle down to market. It is a historic Scottish breed, but its origins are unknown; one theory includes a mix with Polish Sheepdogs brought to Scotland 500 years ago.

Temperament: These are lively, willing workers with bags of stamina, who are friendly and good-tempered. They normally respond well to children. The breed has made a good transfer from working dog to family pet and good companion.

Exercise: Needs time for lots of exercise.

Grooming: The coat demands daily attention.

German Shepherd Dog

Size:
Male
66cm (26in)
40kg (88lb)

Female
60cm (24in)
30kg (65lb)

Commonly known as the Alsatian, today this dog is often first thought of in its role as a police dog; as a result, despite its massive popularity, many people are quite wary of it. Yet its origins are, as its name states, a sheep dog, the Shäferhund.

Temperament: These dogs are intelligent, quick to learn, alert and ever on duty, loyal companions and obedient with a strong, firm owner. If a German Shepherd is to be a housedog, it is essential to socialize and train it well.

Exercise: Needs regular active exercise.

Grooming: A daily brushing is necessary.

Old English Sheepdog

Size:
Male
61cm (24in)
36kg (80lb)

Female
56cm (22in)
30kg (65lb)

This breed is 'old' in the sense that there is visual evidence of its existence over 200 years ago. Although it has been claimed that Russian Sheepdogs (called Owtchah) were crossed with local dogs, in fact a number of European countries, including Britain, had shaggy long-haired sheepdogs and herding dogs, and the Old English Sheepdog was a droving and herding dog.

Temperament: Old English Sheepdogs are cheerful, faithful, calm and biddable. They are generally good with children – as long as they don't knock young ones over. Some breed lines may show a degree of possessiveness.

Exercise: An Old English Sheepdog has a 'bear-like' gait when walking which fits its moderate exercise demands, but will run smoothly.

Grooming: Saving time by not having overlong walks? No, you will use it up and more on the very demanding daily grooming.

The word 'corgi' derives from the Celtic for 'dog'. Two breeds have been registered separately for around 75 years: the Pembroke (born tail-less or docked), right, and the Cardigan (with tail), top left. These dwarf-legged dogs have been used as cattle 'heelers' for many centuries, driving cattle by snapping at their heels, and are thought to be one of the oldest identifiable types in Britain.

Temperament: Corgis are alert and intelligent, and can be trained relatively easily. However, as they have been systematically selected to nip, they are not ideal with young children. (Famously, the Queen's Pembroke Corgis have nipped the ankles of Palace staff throughout her reign.) When Corgis are socialized, they are better with other dogs.

Exercise: Needs moderate exercise.

Grooming: The waterproof coat needs regular brushing.

Welsh Corgi

Size:

Male
31cm (12in)
12kg (26lb)

Female
31cm (12in)
11kg (24lb)

This delightful sheep-herding dog, from the exposed Shetland Islands that lie north of mainland Scotland, is a smaller version of the mainland's Rough Collie. The dogs are to scale with the ponies and sheep that have also become miniaturized with rugged island life. As a convenient size for household living, they have become more common pets than the Collie.

Temperament: These alert, gentle dogs are intelligent and very easily trained. They are sensitive and responsive towards their owners, showing affection, although they may be shy or reserved towards strangers, boisterous children and other dogs.

Exercise: While enjoying a lot of exercise, the dog can adapt and be undemanding as a pet for an older owner.

Grooming: Needs regular brushing, but don't tug with a comb on any matted area. Fortunately, Shelties avoid getting muddy.

Shetland Sheepdog

Size:

Male
37cm (14½1in)
8kg (18lb)

Female
35.5cm (14in)
7kg (161lb)

Looking like a smaller version of the Bearded Collie, in Poland this breed is called the Polski Owezarek Nizinny (Pon). Three Pons were taken from Gdansk to Scotland in 1514 and may have added to the lines forming the Beardie. The breed was nearly destroyed during World War Two, but was saved by a Polish vet, Danuta Hryniewicz.

Temperament: Alert, lively, intelligent and readily trained, these dogs are restrained but effective in herding sheep. The Kennel Club breed standard states: 'perceptive with excellent memory'. Their good nature and size have made them good family dogs.

Exercise: This boisterous dog needs a lot of exercise; however, when not trotting or walking, it changes down a gear into a slow amble.

Grooming: The long, harsh coat and softer undercoat can require a lot of attention.

Polish Lowland Sheepdog

Size:

Male
52cm (20in)
19kg (42lb)

Female
46cm (18in)
19kg (42lb)

23 Non-Sporting and Utility dogs

This is a 'non-group', as there is no reason for a dog to be in this group apart from not fitting into another one! In reality, all Utility dogs have functions that could be slotted into other groups – for instance, the Poodle was originally a water retriever. Breeds that historically were fighting dogs but are not terriers, and small companion dogs that are a bit big for toys have also ended up here.

Shiba Inu

Size:
Male
40cm (16in)
14kg (30lb)

Female
38cm (15in)
13kg (28lb)

This smart-looking Spitz-type dog's name means 'small dog' in Japanese. It originated nearly 2,000 years ago, and was a hunting dog used in catching small game. In 1937 it was identified as a 'Natural Monument', and it is the most popular Japanese dog.

Temperament: As lively and smart as they look, Shiba Inus are independent and can be difficult to train. If owners can be dominated, aggression towards people and other dogs can be the result; however, Shiba Inus enjoy learning with a firm owner and can be sociable.

Exercise: Needs moderate regular exercise.

Grooming: Regular brushing with a firm brush is required.

Dalmatian

Size:
Male
63cm (25in)
29kg (65lb)

Female
60cm (24in)
27kg (60lb)

This was a carriage dog that ran tirelessly along beside its owner, both to give protection and, due to its unique coat, to enhance status. The breed's origins are a mystery: there seems to be no connection with Dalmatia, and the dog is probably the result of a mutation that occurred in England. The coat led to immortalization in Dodie Smith's *101 Dalmatians* and the subsequent Disney films.

Temperament: This exuberant dog is both affectionate and intelligent; its friendly nature – and spots – endear it to children. Dalmatians can be problematic if underexercised, and they need early socialization to dogs and people.

Exercise: Needs lots of long, energetic walks.

Grooming: A daily brushing routine is required.

Lhasa Apso

Size:
26cm (10in)
7kg (15lb)

When Tibet was closed to the rest of the world for centuries, these temple and monastery dogs were only allowed out as gifts from the Dalai Lama in the sacred city of Lhasa, usually only to the Chinese Imperial family. However, in the late 19th century some arrived in England and the breed was recognized by the Kennel Club in 1908. Its Tibetan name is Apso Seng Kye ('Hairy Lion Dog').

Temperament: With their history as companion dogs, Lhasa Apsos enjoy their owner's company, and are alert and readily trained. However, they are reserved with strangers, and need socialization to other dogs when young. They have good hearing and communicate with their owners by sometimes excessive barking

Exercise: Gentle regular exercise is appreciated; the dog is happy to walk, and is robust in the cold,

Grooming: The long topcoat and thick undercoat need regular care.

This occurs in three sizes: Standard, Miniature and Toy. Due to what seem bizarre clips, it is not commonly appreciated that Poodles were bred as hard-working water retrievers: the clip was started to reduce drag at the rear, while leaving some protection at the joints.

Temperament: Poodles are affectionate and respond well to owners, and are known for their intelligence and learning ability, which led to their use in circus troupes. If given socialization, they are normally fine with both strangers and unfamiliar dogs. Standards and Miniatures are good with children, but can exhibit jealousy.

Exercise: The Standard enjoys more exertion than smaller dogs. Their needs are regular but moderate, and they like to play off the lead.

Grooming: Poodles don't shed hair (making them suitable for dog-allergic owners) and thus need regular clipping. Many pet owners go for a simple 'lamb' cut all over.

Poodle
Size:
Standard
over 38cm (15in)
34kg (75lb)

Miniature
under 38cm (15in)
6kg (13lb)

Toy
under 28cm (11in)
4.5kg (10lb)

Born with oversized skin that lies in abundant folds on the pup, Shar Peis gradually almost grow into it by the time they are fully adult. Like the Chow-Chow, the Shar Pei has a black-blue tongue; both breeds are descended from an ancient common ancestor some 2,000 years ago – the Shar Pei was the Chinese Fighting Dog, whose loose skin did not allow an opponent to achieve a proper grip.

Temperament: These dogs are calm and independent, even wilful, but they are generally affectionate. Although they are easygoing, they can have problems with strangers and other dogs, so early socialization is essential.

Exercise: Moderate but regular.

Grooming: While regular brushing is good, the elaborate skin folds can give skin problems and entropion (turned-in eyelids), which can lead to blindness.

Shar Pei
Size:
51cm (20in)
25kg (55lb)

A Miniature Bulldog was developed from the British Bulldog; when this was taken to northern France, it was developed into the French Bulldog, which has pricked, bat-like ears in contrast to the English Miniature's turned-over ears. It gained popularity and a little notoriety as the darling of Paris *demi-mondaine* ladies, and was painted by Toulouse-Lautrec and other artists.

Temperament: Vivacious, good-natured and very affectionate, French Bulldogs are friendly with strangers and, if socialized properly, with other dogs.

Exercise: The breed is undemanding, but don't exercise it too much on hot days.

Grooming: Easy, although the facial folds need regular attention.

French Bulldog
Size:
Male
31cm (12in)
12.5kg (28lb)

Female
26cm (10in)
11kg (24lb)

Toys

This group's name implies 'playthings', which to an extent the dogs have been across history; some breeds have been in existence for thousands of years. When the term 'toy' became formally applied to dog breeds in showing, it purely meant 'very small'; however, a point of distinction for the Toys is that they are the only group bred exclusively as companions – only since the advent of showing have most of the other breeds ceased to be working dogs and followed in the footsteps of the toys.

Cavalier King Charles Spaniel

Size:
32cm (13in)
8kg (18lb)

This is one of the most popular of the Toys. In 17th century England tiny companion spaniels were a fashion accessory at the court of Charles II. During the late 19th century, selection changed the King Charles Spaniel to a flatter-faced form, but in the late 1920s a return to the form of the original began, and the type with a nose of the older style came to be called the Cavalier King Charles Spaniel.

Temperament: Gentle and affectionate, these charming and cheerful, lively little dogs are readily trained. As their history suggests, they make good companions.

Exercise: Needs moderate exercise.

Grooming: The long, silky hair is moderately easy to maintain with comb and brush.

Chinese Crested Dog

Size:
Male
33cm (13in)
up to 5kg (12lb)

Female
30cm (12in)
up to 5kg (12lb)

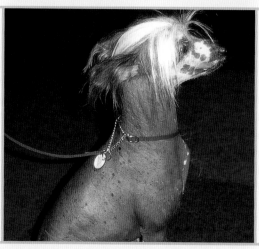

To many people this looks like a weird, space-age designer dog, with an entirely naked body except for long, silky hair at its extremities; yet a dog with this appearance, which may have been brought back from the East, was described in 1686 in the *Natural History of Staffordshire*.

Temperament: Chinese Cresteds are lively and friendly, and like being with people, becoming very attached to their owners. Due to the dog's appearance owners may be tempted particularly to spoil it, which can lead to it becoming snappy with others. (As has been said, 'Despite appearances it is still a dog.')

Exercise: Needs minimal exercise, although it does enjoy a walk. When out it needs sunscreen protection in warm weather and a non-wool coat in the cold.

Grooming: Skin care is necessary.

Chihuahua

Size:
Male
15–23cm (6–9in)
1–3kg (2–6lb)

Female
15–20cm (6–8in)
1–3kg (2–6lb)

Renowned as the world's smallest breed, yet named after an entire Mexican state! That said, is it an Aztec dog (there are small breeds of dog today in Mexico), taken by the Conquistadors, or does it derive from a Chinese miniature? In the 1880s visiting Americans were enamoured and took some home; breed registration occurred in 1903.

Temperament: These bright, spirited dogs don't seem to know they are small. Devoted to their owners, they show affection but can become jealous. They do not seem intimidated by larger dogs, but you need to remember to take extra care around these tiny dogs so as not to harm them. They may shiver if excited or cold.

Exercise: Chihuahuas are undemanding – but you don't need to carry them everywhere!

Grooming: Neither the long-haired nor smooth-coated breeds require much coat care.

While not everyone loves their appearance, Pugs are one of the more popular historic breeds. They were certainly popular by the 17th century, yet the theories about their origins range from ancient Chinese to Russian beginnings.

Temperament: Remarkably even-tempered and sociable, Pugs have a charming, endearing nature and are normally good with children. They enjoy company and don't like being left out, but can be wilful.

Exercise: Needs moderate exercise and enjoys playing games. However, the flattened face can make easy breathing problematic in hot weather. Pugs are naturally stocky, so avoid overfeeding them.

Grooming: Moderate grooming is required.

Pug
Size:
25–28cm (10–11in)
8kg (18lb)

This is found in the American Kennel Club Toy group, the Kennel Club Utility group and the Australian Non-Sporting group. It is thought that Lhasa Apsos sent by the Dalai Lama from Tibet to the Chinese Court were mated there with the Imperial Pekingese. The resultant Shih Tzu had a flatter face than the Tibetan dogs, and was called the Lhasa Lion Dog. Since arriving in the West in the 1930s, the breed has gained incredible popularity.

Temperament: Gentle, friendly, alert and intelligent, Shih Tzus are playful with their owners and respond to training. If socialized when young, they are friendly towards strangers and other dogs.

Exercise: Needs gentle regular exercise; not a fan of walks in cold and mud. Its short muzzle can restrict breathing.

Grooming: Demanding, as the long coat will sweep up mud and bits from outside. The double coat needs regular combing and brushing.

Shih Tzu
Size:
up to 26.7cm (10½in)
5–8kg (10–18lb)

When this tiny and very popular dog is entered for competitions, its combed and brushed hair is so long it is rolled up so it doesn't tangle. Household Yorkies usually have more everyday clips (top left), but can get into other tangles! In Victorian Yorkshire, small Scottish terriers were crossed with local terriers to produce this tiny but indomitable ratter.

Temperament: Yorkies are highly excitable and are likely to be spirited barkers. Even though they are small, they may attack cats and are not readily intimidated by other dogs. With socialization, they are better with strangers and other dogs.

Exercise: Needs little exercise, but barks more when not exercised. Yorkies get a fair bit of exercise in everyday scurrying about.

Grooming: The long skirts of hair are apt to pick up quantities of mud outdoors. Daily grooming is necessary.

Yorkshire Terrier
Size:
up to 23cm (9in)
up to 3.1kg (7lb)

Obedient breeds

In obedience training Doberman Pinschers, Shetland Sheepdogs, Standard and Miniature Poodles and German Shepherds have been found by comparative behaviour ranking by different specialist assessors to score highest, while lowest scores went to Chow Chows, Afghan Hounds, Fox Terriers, English Bulldogs, Basset Hounds and Beagles.

Chow Chows, Afghan Hounds and Fox Terriers have also been scored highest as dogs showing dominance over owners, which is entirely consistent with their poor record for obedience training. Other dogs put in the same bracket of dominance over owners are Scottish Terriers, Miniature Schnauzers and Siberian Huskies.

In contrast, not unexpectedly, Golden Retrievers have been found to show the lowest rank for dominance over owners. Also in the non-dominant ranking are Shetland Sheepdogs and Collies, which have been bred and selected for following the instructions of their owner, plus Brittany Spaniels and Bloodhounds.

Miniature Schnauzers just pip the Golden Retriever at playfulness, but are vastly more excitable. Standard Poodles, which come in the top rank of training, score equally highly at playfulness, but are only moderately excitable. A high obedience rating, coupled with the low reactivity and low aggression of Golden Retrievers, can be found in a group including Labrador Retrievers, Vizslas, Brittany Spaniels, Collies, Newfoundlands and German Shorthaired Pointers.

Of the dogs with the highest capability at obedience and training, German Shepherds, Akitas, Rottweilers and Doberman Pinschers are very low in reactivity but potentially very aggressive, making them effective in police and military work. To achieve this same high degree of trainability, coupled with moderate aggression, the smaller reactive dogs score high, such as Shetland Sheepdogs, Bichon Frises, Welsh Corgis, Shi Tzus and Miniature and Standard Poodles.

In the mid-20th century John Scott and John Fuller systematically compared Basenjis, Beagles, American Cocker Spaniels and Wire-haired Fox Terriers. They found that the ability to respond successfully depended on the type of training, the kind of task and the different characteristics between breeds. They also discovered that the emotional temperament of each breed strongly affected the outcome of the tests and tasks.

Border Collie

Individual character

Breed findings are only a guide – any dog's upbringing, environment, relationship with his owner, past training and genetics within his breed are what form his individuality in obedience and character.

Are some breeds more dominant? 26

Rank order of breed dominance should be considered when choosing a particular breed, particularly as the majority of dominance problems are due to ineffectual efforts of owners to control their dog. If realistically you are going to be unable to play the role of a benign but firm and clear leader to your dog, it is unwise to choose a breed for yourself that is identified as dominant, such as the Chow Chow (right).

If you understand and properly implement good behaviour training of your dog, then any stable dog of a recognized breed can be trained to a reasonable level. Yet this doesn't change the reality that some dogs are more dominant than others, some of which behaviour is down to a breed-based genetic component.

Be realistic when choosing, and remember that more dogs die in their first couple of years as a result of being put to death for 'behavioural problems' than as a result of illness or road accidents – most of those problems are due to lack of proper training, usually arising from the owner's inability to cope with a dog displaying dominance or aggression. A household where the dog is more dominant than all the humans is uncomfortable and probably unsafe.

But this need not happen, and making better informed choices in the first place for what breed is appropriate for you is a good start; making a proper amount of time available for training and carrying out a proper programme of training ensures that your dog will trust you as its leader.

HOW DOES MY DOG RATE?

In extensive surveys of obedience judges and veterinarians by renowned behaviourists Benjamin and Lynette Hart, and of breeders by Dr Daniel Tortora, a comparable ranking emerged.

Obedience training low-scorers

Chow Chows
Afghan Hounds
Fox Terriers
English Bulldogs
Basset Hounds
Beagles

Obedience training high-scorers

Doberman Pinschers
Shetland Sheepdogs
Standard and Miniature Poodles
German Shepherds

Dominant high-scorers

Chow Chows
Afghan Hounds
Fox Terriers
Scottish Terriers
Miniature Schnauzers
Siberian Huskies

Dominant low-scorers

Golden Retrievers
Shetland Sheepdogs
Collies
Brittany Spaniels
Bloodhounds

Dominance over owners is but one aspect of an aggressive potential, which can be seen in aggression to other dogs and people, and as territorial defensiveness; and it is a key factor that will certainly affect training. Some dogs, such as German Shepherds, Doberman Pinschers and Rottweilers, have a particularly high aggressive potential, but in proper hands they can achieve a very high level of training. In contrast, some dogs may rate low in general aggression, including English Bulldogs, Basset Hounds and Old English Sheepdogs, but these are also low scorers on trainability!

Siberian Huskies

The Golden Rule – get the basics right

If you are encountering dominance problems, the key to making this far less of an issue is proper training, especially ensuring that the basics are in place.

Biters

Dog pounds, shelters and vets are the dumping ground for biting dogs, reflecting a situation where there has been behavioural breakdown due to lack of habituation, proper training and proper behaviour by owners towards their dogs.

According to recent studies in the USA, in one year in Baltimore there were over 7,000 animal bites reported, of which 6,800 were by dogs. In Pittsburgh, out of nearly 1,000 dog bites in one year, 39 per cent were to legs, 37 per cent to arms, 16 per cent to heads, faces and necks.

Another recent study found that 91 per cent of dog bites occurring within family households do not get seen by a doctor. This is good, in that it implies that most bites are not physically too damaging, but also very concerning, in that it means that dog bites are massively under-recorded, and in consequence a real idea of the number occurring is hard to establish.

What should you do if you find your dog is aggressive to people and nips or escalates to biting others? The American Dog Trainers Network's number one action is: 'Remove rose-coloured glasses.' This is really good advice, for the first reaction of most owners is to go into denial and pretend that what is happening is not happening. If you have a puppy, make sure that he is socialized; for an adult biter, check the sections on aggression towards people on pages 100–102.

If your dog bites, realize that complaints from those bitten or others can result in the dog being destroyed. Most bites happen to family, friends and neighbours, and occur in aggressive actions for a wide variety of reasons. In the USA estimates of dog bites range from 0.5–5,000,000 a year, while the yearly number reported is 1,000,000; there are some 12–15 fatalities from dog bites each year.

As there is a sliding scale of biting, from pups' safe, inhibited mouthing to rare fatalities, many owners do not know when to seek help with a biting dog. It is natural for pups to mouth objects, including hands, but when teeth become larger your pup needs feedback; a loud 'Aah!' or 'Ouch!' sets needed boundaries. If there is any doubt, call in a dog trainer or behaviourist for an assessment.

Threats to, or punishment of strongly dominant dogs can result in biting. If your dog bites because of dominance aggression, professional advice may be to have him neutered (see page 77).

It is easy to be bitten through redirected aggression by intervening in dog fights, or for another dog or person to be bitten when a dog defends his home against something outside and the aggression is redirected on to others. Play aggression's inhibited nips can escalate, and bites can also result from both owner and dog misreading the signs and misunderstanding the situation – most misunderstandings occur over wary or fearful behaviour, from which fear biting can arise as a last-ditch defence by a dog when his clear submissive signs have been ignored (see pages 26–29).

Staffordshire Bull Terrier

Biting breeds
The general bite risk has been found highest in Pit Bull Terriers, Chow Chows, German Shepherds, Dobermans and Rottweilers.

For considerations of safety with children, breeds have been ranked by specialist assessors, and those least likely to snap at children were found to be reliable Golden Retrievers and incredibly popular Labrador Retrievers; Newfoundlands, Bloodhounds, Basset Hounds and Collies also scored highly.

Boxer

It is considered that the most likely breed to snap at children is the little Pomeranian, closely followed by Yorkshire Terriers, which certainly have a wide reputation for being snappy. Chow Chows score badly, as do West Highland White Terriers, Miniature Schnauzers and Scottish Terriers.

In a study made in Baltimore, USA, 60 per cent of people bitten were under 15 years of age, yet this age group made up under 30 per cent of the population; similar findings have been found at other cities. The highest risk of being a victim is the age group for children aged 5–9, and boys are twice as likely to be bitten as girls. Most bites occurred near the owner's home. It was found that 66 per cent of the attacks were directly provoked by the victim or by the child playing, and the rest were apparently unprovoked. To put all this into perspective, around 1 per cent of children taken to emergency medical aid require treatment for dog bites.

These figures dramatically underline the need for owners not only to appreciate the need to train their dogs and to keep them under control, but also to show that their dogs see them as pack leaders normally and behave accordingly. However, when we are out of sight our dogs do not have the same degree of inhibition, and the domesticated wolf asserts its rank position. The real problem lies in households where the human adults do not have proper control of the dog or dogs, which assume that they are dominant to the adults – here the relative rank of the children is much lower, so they become more at risk.

There are two clear reasons why children, especially boys, are at most risk of being bitten. One is that children, especially boys, spend a higher percentage of play time with dogs than adults, and in the competitive rough and tumble of ball games they try to pull things away from dogs' mouths. The second is the ambiguity of rank position in our households. Children are not viewed by dogs as having the same authority as adults: they are smaller, often tumble about on the ground and have higher-pitched voices than adults.

If children become concerned by a dog's behaviour they should stand up, thereby increasing their dominance and decreasing the risk of being bitten. Not surprisingly, children of 4 or younger who have been bitten receive injuries to the face, but as children get older and taller, this is dramatically reduced.

Reducing the risks

- Don't leave young children alone with dogs, particularly groups of dogs.
- Teach children how to behave properly and safely with dogs.
- Assume the responsibility of a proper relationship with household dogs.
- Make sure all dogs are thoroughly socialized and trained.

Cocker
Spaniel

The nose

As scent molecules are trapped by moisture and mobilized to detection sites, the value to the dog of having a moist nose and long snout are incalculable – and it explains the mystery of why healthy dogs have cold wet noses. Breeds such as Bloodhounds have exaggerated this with broad, long noses, and we utilize dogs' sense of smell in everything from drug detection to finding truffles.

The external black wet nosepad is called the rhinarium. The nasal cavity is divided by a nasal septum, and inside each chamber are bony and cartilaginous plates called turbinals, which are like radiator fins covered with a membrane. In the Dog family the turbinals are in complicated foldings to give a large surface area: as air is breathed in, it warms as it passes over these plates, and also becomes moister. The membrane containing the olfactory cells is not throughout the nose, but just at the back, receiving the air after it has been warmed.

The nasal cavity of different breeds of dog varies dramatically, from flatter-faced (or brachycephalic) dogs, such as Pekingese or British Bulldogs, to long-nosed (or dolichocephalic) breeds, such as Greyhounds or Borzois. Unfortunately, the distortions of the nostrils in brachycephalic noses prevent dilation during breathing : inhalation can become impossible, forcing these dogs to breathe through their mouths (see Inherited Problems, page 126).

The significance of scent to dogs compared to us is reflected in dogs' ability to detect odours at very low concentrations. While humans can detect down to 4.5–10 Molar, dogs can show reactions to smells that are at much lower concentrations of 10–17 Molar. The dog has been shown to have different sensitivities of detection to different molecule components of smells.

The incredible facility of dogs to detect and identify one specific scent amid others was recently highlighted in a preliminary report of a Californian study in spring 2006, which showed that trained dogs had a high success rate in detecting patients with lung cancer by smelling their breath, but not quite as good an ability with breast cancer patients. This amazing detection ability of dogs is made possible by receptor cells in the nasal membrane that detect different scents, so a distinct set of olfactory receptors is used for each specific scent.

Dogs used in police line-ups to identify criminals from crime scene scent have about a 75 per cent success rate, while field success in tracking is 93–100 per cent.

Dogs are able to interpret sexual scents, which they undertake when meeting and greeting other dogs. They have a similar facitily with other species: they have been recorded as having over 80 per cent success in detecting cows in oestrus, and we all know dogs' behaviour in directly sniffing out information on human visitors!

Dogs interpret sexual scents via a separate scent-detecting organ, the Jacobson's or vomero-nasal organ, located above the roof of the mouth in the bony forward section of the nasal septum. If you spot your dog with his mouth held slightly ajar and a focused look on his face, he is using this organ.

Mongrel

The powerful nose

The olfactory membrane of a human nose is around 3cu cm (³⁄₁₆ cu in), while the importance of its sense of smell to a dog can be realized from it having around 130cu cm (8cu in), depending on the breed. Some breeds have far more olfactory sensory cells: for example, German Shepherds have almost twice those of some Terriers, and 45 times as many as a human being.

Many owners think of their dogs as purely daytime animals, but while they may not have the degree of nocturnal specialization of the cat family, dogs do have good night and day vision.

Dandy Dinmont

BREEDS WITH POTENTIAL EYE PROBLEMS

English Cocker Spaniels, Siberian Huskies, Pekingese, Miniature Long-haired Dachshunds, Shetland Sheepdogs, Border Collies, Labrador Retrievers, Rough and Smooth Collies, Golden Retrievers, English Springer Spaniels, Briards, Elkhounds, Irish Setters, Miniature, Toy and Standard Poodles, Afghan Hounds, Chow Chows, Shar Peis, Jack Russell Terriers, German Shepherds, West Highland White Terriers, Cavalier King Charles Spaniels, Miniature Schnauzers, Staffordshire Bull Terriers, Boston Terriers, American Cocker Spaniels and others.

As a hunting animal, the wolf and its descendant the dog have forward-pointing eyes; depending on the breed, dogs' eyes have an area of binocular vision in the overlap field from their eyes of some 60–16°. The amount of visual overlap between the eyes gives binocular vision, which enables a better appreciation of depth of field for the hunting dog to detect its prey. The dog naturally has excellent vision, with the forward-facing eyes of a hunter providing good depth of field.

Genetically inherited eye disorders are both numerous and relatively common among certain dog breeds, and potential owners need to be alert to this. Don't just fall for the pup because it's cute – check that the breeders have the correct certification to show that the puppy should be free of any inherited eye conditions. In addition, flat-faced breeds tend to have had their tear drainage (nasolacrimal) ducts buckled by breeding, so tears tend to flow down the face rather than draining properly into the nose.

The eyelids don't only act as light shades, also protect the eye from damage, spreading the film of tears that can wash away particles. The third eyelid, also known as the haw or nictitating membrane, acts as a protective shutter that slides across sideways underneath the other eyelids at times of danger to the eye; it can be seen protruding in the inner corner of the eye. Tears arise from the lacrimal or tear gland located below the upper eyelid; and there is a further, smaller tear gland at the base of the third eyelid.

Just as in a camera, the iris, the coloured ring in the eye that we can see surrounding the central dark aperture, or pupil, fulfils the role of a diaphragm in controlling the amount of light that enters the eye. It is not just the external amount of light that affects this size, but also the mood of the dog: if he is fearful, the pupil widens to give a better peripheral awareness, which allows him to better anticipate an attack from the side. If the dog is aggressive and about to attack, the pupil reduces in size, giving better precision of sight from an improved depth of field.

As light enters the eye it is focused on to the retina as it passes through the lens. Dogs have more rods than cones as photoreceptors in their retinas, sacrificing some daytime colour reception in favour of a better ability to see at low light levels.

31 The ears

Dogs can hear over a wider range of frequencies than can humans, and their good high frequency hearing has been utilized by shepherds' 'silent' whistles. But it may come as a surprise to dog owners, and especially shepherds, that dogs have been found to not be as sensitive at high frequencies as cats. Dogs' clearest hearing is over the range 200–15,000Hz, but if loud enough, sounds below 20Hz can be heard.

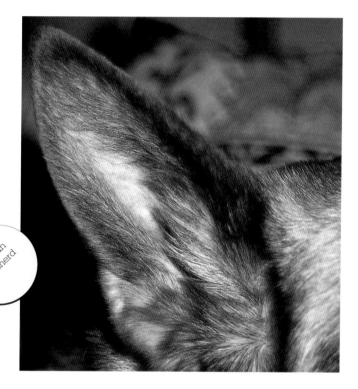

German Shepherd

Good hearing was invaluable to the hunting wolf ancestors of the dog, and breeds that have been selected to exaggerate the dependence on hearing have retained pricked ears, such Huskies, Basenjis, German Shepherds, Collies and Corgis. Despite this, the majority of dogs have been bred with flop ears, including Mastiffs, Old English Sheepdogs, Dalmatians, Jack Russell Terriers, Airedale Terriers, Spaniels, Basset Hounds and Bloodhounds. They have reduced ability to focus the pinnae for sound analysis, yet most dogs have some ability to move their ears, based on a system of 17 muscles. Pricked-ear dogs can focus their attention to the source of a sound to a width of 4° by the movement of the pinnae. The pricking-up of the ears in response to a sound is called the Preyer's reflex, but this is less consistent at low sounds under 8,000Hz than above.

While the ear pinnae of those breeds needing to hear well are erect, flop ears can be behaviourally misread as submissive. Not only are flopped-over ears a problem for dog signalling, but they increase the risk of wax accumulation and otitis externa, which brings head scratching, inflammation and discomfort.

The dog's ear can be considered as having three parts: the visible part, the pinna, is the external ear. The ear canal inside it has glands that produce the ear wax. With the ancestral wolf-type pricked ear, the wax dries naturally as it moves up the canal near to the outside, where it is shaken away, but this does not occur in floppy-eared dogs, who need to be monitored for hearing problems from blocked wax.

At the middle ear, the end of the auditory canal is covered across by a membrane, the eardrum. The outer ear brings air vibration to this drum, and its vibrations are passed on through three small bones to an inner drum, and the sound waves reach the inner ear. Here they travel through a fluid-filled spiral called the cochlea, in which vibration receptors transmit the signals along nerves to the brain. Also lodged in the inner ear are the fluid-filled semi-circular canals that detect which way up the dog is positioned, conveying a sense of balance – for an animal that rushes about so much, an acute awareness of balance is invaluable.

Basset Hound

A clear indication that, among carnivores, the dog family is both more of a scavenger and prepared to encompass a wider range of foods than the cat family is the 'sweet tooth' only too often displayed by our dogs!

German Shepherd

The dog's tongue has numbers of papillae, bumps, some of which are home to specialist nerve endings, called 'taste buds'. Four pairs of salivary glands duct saliva to the tongue and mouth, where it not only lubricates the food and begins the digestion process, but also revives flavour from dry foods. In the dog's tongue are fibre receptors that respond to sweet, bitter, acidic and salt flavours; dogs are omnivorous carnivores, while cats, which are obligate carnivores, show very little responsiveness to sweetness.

Hunters that only eat prey do not become exposed to sweet tastes, and sweetness in nature is restricted in dietary form to ripened fruit, honey in bees' nests and rich nectaries of some species of flower. Wolves will eat berries, but not as a significant part of their diets; jackals are regular scavengers and eat seasonal fruits, and are known as raiders of fruit crops; coyotes and foxes readily scavenge and also eat significant quantities of seasonal fruit – in the autumn, in fact, this can be their major source of food.

THE TASTE GATE

Access to the digestive system is by the mouth, and taste is the key to that gate. It allows preferred foods and bars others.

Food toxins can be bitter, and dogs are sensitive to such tastes. Their sweet-detecting taste buds, which are located at the hind section of the tongue, react positively to natural sugars; artificial sweeteners, such as saccharine, have a bitter quality that causes dogs to avoid them. Dogs' taste buds favour amino acids and nucleotides, both of which are components of meat.

Salt is important for life – half of a goat's taste receptors are there to detect it.

However, dogs have poor salt detection by comparison because, as carnivores, their diet contains a natural balance of salt. As dogs get older, their taste buds become less sensitive.

Dogs' taste prefers meat to plantstuffs, and discrimination of the type of meat involves smell and taste; they prefer beef to chicken. Although they like fatty food, they dislike rancid fat.

In dogs, taste aversion can be learned as a conditioned response – if a particular food has made a dog sick, the dog then usually avoids it.

If your dog loses his appetite when he is unwell, gently warm his food a little, which helps him to be able to taste and smell it.

33 Diet

Although dogs are carnivores, they are happy to eat a diet not wildly different from our own, but with a bit more protein – a balance of protein, carbohydrates and fats, plus vitamins (A, B group, D and E), minerals, fibre and, of course, water.

Boxer

Water

A small dog, such as a Pekingese or Papillon, needs an intake of water (from all sources) of about 200ml a day; a middle-size dog, such as an Irish Setter or Golden Retriever, needs around 1,200ml; and a big dog, such as a St Bernard, will take up in excess of 2l. All dogs need more water in hot weather.

It is quite easy to give a dog a reasonably balanced diet from home, but commercially produced dog foods that are nutritionally balanced have the advantage of convenience and should have the correct balance of vitamins, minerals and other components. Foods labelled as, complete, do not need the addition of biscuits to alter the protein balance, but tinned meat does.

Try to match the amount of food you give daily to produce the ideal weight for the breed. When using commercial dog food, always read and follow the guidelines. Remember that dry and semi-moist complete foods do not have the same quantity of water as a tinned complete food. In addition, there isn't as much water as you might expect in a semi-moist dog food compared to a dry food; compared to a tinned complete food, both are missing most of their volume, which the dog will take on when it drinks water. As a rough guide, it is advisable to give only about 40 per cent of the weight of the correct amount of a complete tinned food – if you feed such water-reduced foods in the same quantities, your dog will put on weight rapidly. Dogs cannot fully digest vegetable protein, so too much water in a mix can cause digestive problems.

FOOD AND BEHAVIOUR

If you or your family dole out food at mealtimes, then your dog can become a real pain, begging and demanding. This is also one of the main contributing factors in undermining an owner's ability to control a dog, and accentuates the problems with dominant dogs.

Leaving food down all the time for your dog is very bad news for his ability to control his toilet habits. If you are having fouling problems with your dog, feeding in this manner may be a key reason.

Feed your dog only at specified times, and then only leave the food down for 20 minutes or so. This becomes a great incentive for him to eat at that time. His digestion will then have a set timetable, and he will want to relieve himself at a particular time. Try to ensure that his feeding time produces his elimination time at a time when you normally take him for a walk.

Diet is another field in which dogs' pack-animal ancestry asserts itself: their forerunners, wolves, had to eat quickly to consume food before others in the pack ate their share. For this reason, don't be tempted to overfeed your dog when he rapidly empties his plate and lets you know that he wants more, as this can lead to problems with obesity, described in more detail on page 137.

The dog's digestive system breaks down food and water intake from complex proteins, carbohydrates and fats into component molecules that are of a size and form that can be absorbed into the body.

Digestion starts with the teeth: at the side of the mouth dogs have stabbing canines and premolars and molars that chew and grind. The front incisors are for more precise cutting off of meat from around bones in small movements. A diet of soft foods can lead to tartar build-up due to lack of proper chewing; however, access to hard biscuits and rawhide chews helps to combat tartar accumulation.

Gradually introducing your dog to the use of a toothbrush can be advantageous. The main reason for tooth loss in dogs is periodontal disease from plaque and bacteria, which is accompanied by bad breath or halitosis, and drooling.

The breakdown of the foodstuffs is facilitated by enzymes exuded at various parts of the digestive system starting at the salivary glands in the mouth, where amylase begins the digestion of carbohydrates. The gastric juices of the stomach continue the process, and once the small intestine is reached further enzymes continue the action on proteins, carbohydrates and fats. Bile from the gall bladder emulsifies the fats so they can be absorbed through the gut wall.

The bolus of food from the mouth the stomach, and from that along the small intestine, is moved by peristaltic muscle waves. Proteins are rendered into their component amino acids, and carbohydrates into their component sugars. These smaller molecules are readily absorbed along with water by the small intestine. The large intestine absorbs water.

Pups in competition with each other will eat up to 50 per cent more when fed alone; however, as mentioned opposite, this tendency for dogs to eat more than they need – purely because the food is there in front of them – can lead to weight problems. That said, dogs have feedback controls that can be affected by you: dogs that are warm tend to eat less than those who are cold, so feeding your dog in a warm room will mean that he eats less. A strict regime of not feeding from the table, feeding leftovers in addition to his normal meals, or giving treats is also helpful in both keeping the dog's weight down and aiding his digestive system.

DIGESTIVE PROBLEMS

Diarrhoea is common in dogs: rotting foods are usually the cause, and the problem normally only lasts a few days. Other causes range from poisons to potentially fatal canine parvovirus, which produces blood in watery faeces, when the vet should be contacted; a more chronic form of diarrhoea accompanied by gradual weight loss can be due to an underactive pancreas. However, diarrhoea is often caused by your dog not being suited to a particular food, and another could match better.

Simple acute gastritis is very common in dogs, in large part due to their being drawn to foul-smelling food, and eating faeces and bones; in consequence, vomiting is a safety valve that can save your dog not only discomfort but even its life. When pups vomit, this is often a reflex to the inexperienced bolting of food – a hangover from when packs caught food and one dog would be in competition with others. In older dogs, however, don't assume that your dog will vomit up foul materials; if you are concerned, consult your vet.

Due to their liking for sweet tastes, dogs will overeat sweet foods, so avoid giving your dog cake – usually not the dog's fault so much as ours.

Cavalier King Charles Spaniel

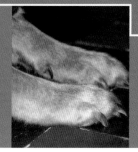

Activity

The exercise needs of dogs vary hugely. Hounds and gundogs tend to eat heartily to allow for long running, and can put on weight easily if they become less active. Terriers are lively and don't go in for gorging, which may help their longevity. The Utility bunch are a ragbag assortment, so looking for a pattern is a non-starter. The Working breeds are hardworking, with a tendency to want to work and take charge. Toys are small and have a small intake, but can be very lively.

Veterinary behavioural scientist Benjamin Hart of Davis University, California, assembled a comparative rank order for activity among the 56 breeds most frequently registered by the American Kennel Club. The rank order was divided into 10 groups, or deciles, of increasing activity. The highest and lowest groups were found to be:

Lowest: Basset Hound, Bloodhound, Bulldog, Newfoundland, Collie, St Bernard

Highest: West Highland White Terrier, Irish Terrier, Fox Terrier, Miniature Schnauzer, Chihuahua, Silky Terrier

The short-legged Basset Hound, which has the distinction of being considered the least active among popular dogs, is facially similar to the next up on the list, the Bloodhound, because one breed is a 'parent' of the other. Son of the Victorian painter, Sir Everett Millais crossed the existing French Basset with a Bloodhound in the first recorded case of artificial insemination in dogs.

In another study Lynette and Benjamin Hart contrasted nine particular characteristics linked to the Basset's low activity with the same characteristics of the Miniature Schnauzer from the highest activity group, with 10 being the highest profile and 1 the lowest. From the result in the table below it is easy to see how different their metabolic and behaviour characteristics are from each other.

Chihuahua & Basset Hound

Characteristic	Basset Hound	Miniature Schnauzer
Activity	1	10
Excitability	1	10
Snapping at children	1	10
Excessive barking	4	10
Territorial defence	1	10
Dominance over owner	3	10
Aggression to dogs	4	10
Playfulness	1	10
Destructiveness	2	8

'Oh, he's as daft as a brush – he runs madly about and then flops down and pants like a steam engine!' This exasperated yet affectionate comment from an owner, describing her dog's approach to life, neatly sums up the dog's approach to temperature control.

Mammals are homeothermic – they retain and control body heat so that they can optimize their metabolism – unlike 'cold-blooded' reptiles, whose activity is largely controlled by their environment's temperature. Different species of mammal have different mechanisms to deal with a common need: we humans are naturally nearly nude animals and have little hair to retain heat, but instead we have many sweat glands in our skin, which aid cooling by evaporation of sweat. Our early history was in warm climates where losing heat was important, but we are less good at retaining heat.

In contrast, dogs and cats are both furred, but the cat is a dash sprinter, whose strategy is to avoid becoming too hot by not running for very long. The dog, however, is a distance runner and thus is less conservative about heat. Dogs have excellent blood vessel supply to their muscles, which avoids lactic acid build-up and the runner's enemy, cramp. Haemoglobin-rich blood in dogs' abundant blood vessels brings in oxygen and removes carbon dioxide and lactate.

Dogs do not sweat on to their fur, otherwise the dramatic heat loss would be problematic; the only skin area from which they can sweat is via their footpads. Instead they pant hard, which cools them by losing heat. However, their skin capillaries do dilate, like ours, to radiate heat. Consequently dogs with thicker coats find it harder to lose heat.

For all these reasons large, round, thickly furred dogs are likely to suffer significantly from heat effects caused by vigorous exercise or being trapped in a hot environment such as a car left in the sun. The dog is vulnerable to overheating and heatstroke, and fat dogs suffer particularly badly in the heat, which is another good reason to protect your dog against obesity.

Panting fast to cool down might seem counterproductive, as the action produces heat! Yet that steam-train panting is at the same resonant frequency of the lungs, so less energy is used. As long as the dog has access to water, panting is an efficient mechanism, even in warm conditions, with air drawn in at the nose, where heat is lost initially by evaporation.

Rottweiler

Hot Dogs!

Dogs naturally operate at a higher temperature than ourselves: our body's temperature is optimal at 37°C (98.6°F), while a dog's is 38.6°C (101.5°F). In general, larger and rounder dogs retain heat more than smaller and thinner dogs, which are better radiators with a larger surface-area-to-volume ratio.

Dog vs cat

As key carnivores, dogs and cats share a few features, such that they both lack good salt detection, and both are unable to focus their eyes on objects when they are close. However, the cat as a lone hunter is a specialist, while the dog as a group hunter is a generalist – as a cog in the machine of the pack there has not been the selection pressure to specialize (although human selection pressures have developed specialist breeds).

Feral dog & cats, Thailand

Dogs share with wolves the stamina that confers the ability to run down prey. Dogs share with sprint-running cats a reduction in the collar bone that endows the animals with a mobile shoulder joint position, allowing them to extend their stride to advantage in a chase. Most carnivores have a mobile fibula, especially cats, but not dogs – *Canidae* are cursorial: their ankle moves in one plane just like a hinge and has no flexible lateral movement. The lower end of the fibula is strongly bound to the tibia to give great stability at the expense of flexibility. This allows the dog to have sustained running, but makes it hopeless for climbing – a dog may chase fast after a cat, but if the cat reaches a tree it can escape up it, leaving the dog behind.

The small clavicles found in most carnivores is entirely absent in the dog family, as dog's don't rotate their forelimbs and so don't need it. The shoulder blade in climbing cats is fan-shaped for broad muscle attachment, but for running dogs it is more efficient to have long narrow scapulas, which give greater stride length.

Compared to the very specialized proctractible mechanism of the cat's claws, the lack of flexibility of the dog's paw makes it seem non-specialized at first sight. Far from it, however: the feet and legs of the dog – like those of its ancestors, wolves, jackals and so on – are a key specialized area for lengthy pursuit as a pack.

Dogs have feet that are adapted to long-distance running on their toes (digitigrades). Their leg muscles are fed with a significant quantity of blood vessels (much greater than those of sprinting cats), as continuous running requires a constant supply of oxygen and nutrients, and removal of carbon dioxide and lactate. In the dog this is also aided by its quantity of haemoglobin-containing red blood cells; this was noted by dog biologists Raymond and Lorna Coopinger as being especially important in the specialist running breeds of the sled dogs and Greyhounds.

To tell a dog's footprint from a cat's, look for the imprint of claws, which are missing from cats' prints. The dog's broad claws are fixed in position to assist grip in continuous running, and are consequently blunted through use. In contrast, the cat's sheathed claws stay sharp for climbing and capturing their prey.

Dogs have longer generalist muzzles, and have more generalized teeth than the cat, which is consistent with the dog's more omnivorous diet of meat and plants. Linked to this, the dog's taste buds are triggered by sugars that occur in a diet with plant materials. Unlike cats, dogs regurgitate food for pups, and are able to do this as they have a coat of muscle over the stomach and oesophagus. The caecum of dogs is larger than that of cats or other carnivores, which is what allows them to be omnivorous carnivores. Bacterial fermentation also takes place in the large intestine of dogs, from which they gain released fatty acids.

Dogs have an inter-ramal tuft of whiskers under their chins, which the cat's specialized, flatter face has lost. The dog is able to gain significant information from these whiskers to adjust head height when scent-tracking prey fast.

Hunting, chasing and herding

A pack of wolves streaming together down a hillside, in pursuit of prey such as deer or caribou, wheel and turn in as co-ordinated a manner as a flock of coastal wading birds. To move as other animals do, to keep running with other animals in companion movement is an essential requirement for pack hunting. The term for this group action is allelomimetic behaviour, and this has been directly inherited by dogs.

Border Collie & sheep

A pack can pursue large animals, and typically 15 or so wolves will select out weaker runners to pick on; if a larger prey item vigorously defends itself, it is usually passed over for another. In the course of making this selection, the pack will turn a herd of grazing animals this way and that – a type of movement of mobilizing herds that in an inhibited form is retained in sheepdogs.

It is sometimes thought that sheepdogs have to be low in aggression, yet they need sufficient aggressive drive to pursue sheep, simultaneously being trained enough to be instantly controlled by the handler. Larger herding dogs that were also used for cattle as well as sheep were normally developed as protecting dogs, and needed to be able to return aggression.

As the desire to chase and hunt is within the dog's behaviour pattern, this is something that dog owners need to address. Owners often enjoy taking their dogs for walks across farmland footpaths, and because it is away from the road traffic, they often release their dog from its leash. In arable fields this is usually not a problem, but where there is livestock the dog should be on a leash to ensure control (see page 82).

Similarly, some breeds chase after cars and bikes, endangering themselves and others, while many will chase after a retreating cat. While a faceful of claws from a cornered cat may dissuade the dog from anything further, these 'hunting scenes' in the urbanized world need to be tempered by training.

Wolves are not particularly fast compared to some prey, but have stamina for persistence, which the dog has inherited, and shows in the readiness of most dogs for long walks. Wolves will normally abandon pursuit in the face of strong resistance, but the selection of dogs in the terrier group of breeds has been to continue an attack almost despite any resistance.

When a prey animal has been separated from a group in the wild, if it is large the back legs are normally attacked first, then the rumps and flank, and finally one wolf grabs the nose. While most breeds of dogs would behave in a similar manner in such a situation, the Bulldog was selected for its tendency to grab the bull's nose and hang on with its powerful jaws, even before its modification to its present form, which has greatly reduced its facility for pursuing its prey.

Courtship

Essentially the courtship and mating undergone by the domestic dog is the same as for the ancestral wolf or, as here, the African Wild Dog. Sexual behaviour only normally takes place when the female is receptive in oestrus, and, as with most mammals, hormones released from the pituitary cause the ovaries to form and release eggs.

When the female (or bitch) comes into heat, this normally lasts about 18 days. The first half of this time is called pro-oestrus, during which she begins to attract the interest of male dogs, but she is not yet sexually receptive, and although she may be coquettish, she rejects any advances.

On entering oestrus she does become receptive, and she may be so for days, during which time mating may be repeated many times; there is a fertile window of about five days. During courtship the male sniffs the female's head and vulva, and she reciprocates. Both animals may at times extend their forepaws along the ground, keeping their rump raised. They can become playful, embracing the other's neck with their forepaws. This behaviour pattern is seen in both dogs and wolves.

However, there are differences: domestication allows the females to become sexually mature towards the end of their first year, while this does not happen for another one or two years in wolves. Most bitches may come into season twice a year, while 'primitive' Basenjis, wolves and African Wild Dogs do so only once. In the wild pack canids – wolves and African Wild Dogs – normally only the alpha male and female mate, and the rest of the pack act as 'helpers'.

African Wild Dogs

When the female (domestic or wild) becomes ready for mating, she will normally present her rear to the male with her tail aside. He mounts her, gripping her sides with his forelegs, positions and inserts his penis, and thrusts rhythmically.

The bitch's seasonal cycle is under hormonal control, the hormones being produced by the development of eggs in her ovaries. Each egg grown is surrounded by supporting cells that produce oestrogen, which causes the womb walls to thicken and the external vulva to swell. During pro-oestrus the female exudes a bloody discharge (this is not menstruation). When ripe, the eggs are released from the ovaries over two or three days, and the support cells left behind now produce progesterone; the dog's discharge ceases, and she becomes keen to accept male attention.

Tied together

Once they have mated, or are interrupted, paired dogs cannot separate. In a mechanism that is unique to the *Canidae* once intromission happens, the *bulbus glandis* of the male's penis swells up and locks them together. Why should this happen has long been a puzzle, as it seemingly makes the animals vulnerable to attack at a critical time.

It has been suggested that the copulatory tie allows time for copulation to occur, but that is really putting the cart before the horse, for copulation time in species is readily adapted to other circumstances, and such an elaborate lock would only lead to more significant requirements.

A number of species of mammal have adapted penises, but the most revealing comparison is with the cat family. The more solitary cat is fiercely territorial and needs a mechanism to allow time for males to gather. The male's penis has barbs which trigger the female to release her eggs only after mating has taken place.

The dog family has the reverse problem to overcome, and this is achieved by the copulatory tie. As a pack animal the domestic dog's wolf ancestor usually had competing mates already on hand, and once mated, the tie prevents another male mounting for anything up to an hour.

When the male dog first mounts the female and makes typical mating thrusts, he usually ejaculates a nearly sperm-free liquid. To humans it may seem strange that this early mating occurs without an erect penis, but, unlike humans, the dog's penis contains a bone (os penis) which enables penetration. As thrusting becomes more vigorous the penis swells, and the *bulbus glandis* locks the male and female together. Only then does the male ejaculate sperm.

The male usually attempts to dismount, but due to the lock, male and female stand back to back. This move seems to make a rotation restriction, slowing the rate of blood drainage. The pair may stay locked by the tie for up to half an hour, and during this time a further clear ejaculate washes the sperm along the female's uterus. As the volume of the sperm ejaculate is small and deposited in the lower vagina, this third, washing ejaculate is important in ensuring fertilization, and can only occur if the dogs are locked.

Normally bitches have a high success rate in becoming pregnant, and from mating to whelping takes around 63 days. For the first few days after the eggs are fertilized, they do not settle or attach to the womb; instead, the embryo develops utilizing the nutrition stored in a yolk sac, and when the embryos do connect to the uterine wall they position in rows. Once placental contact is made, the embryo takes its nourishment from the mother.

In general, developing pups become detectable in the abdomen from around the fifth week, although a vet can usually diagnose their presence from about three and a half weeks after mating. At about this time the mammary glands begin to enlarge.

During pregnancy it is necessary to gradually increase the bitch's food; get advice from your vet about calcium and other supplements to be added to the food. At this time your dog should also be taking some steady exercise, and you should prepare a whelping box or set aside a specific area that can be used for the birth.

Don't interfere

Never try to separate tied mating dogs, as this will damage the sexual organs of both animals. If you are witness to the unplanned mating of your pedigree bitch, consult your vet to avoid further developments.

4

Training the growing dog

Golden
Retriever pups

Pup development

Pups are born with a nervous system that is far from fully developed, and so they are very dependent upon their mother's care. As Labradors and Retrievers are the most popular breed grouping, here I'm following the development of Golden Retriever pups – although exact timings vary with breeds, the pattern is similar. The pups pictured right are just two days old.

Week 1
Neonatal Phase

Pups have broad, 'blob' faces, with sealed eyes and ears.
Face, nose, and feet are baby pink in the first couple of days.

Pups lie with their heads flat to the ground, or lie across litter mates.
They have little ability to really lift their head.

Newborn pups have a 'rooting reflex' to find a teat by pushing their head towards warmth.
This reflex keeps them close to the mother or in a heap with their siblings. Initially a pup has poor control over temperature, so this protection is essential. Pups have a sense of taste from birth, albeit not a full adult capability, but this encourages them to suckle; in the first few days suckling takes up nearly a third of their time. Pups have touch sensitivity on their face so they can feel their way to food.

A young pup will swing its head in reflex actions if you touch its flank or face.
These actions allow it to struggle through the mound of litter mates. However, very young pups do not have the strength in their limbs to move about much or support their body, and life is a round of suckling and sleeping. If they fall out of the nest they cannot get back by themselves, but their distress calls bring mother, who lifts them back in. The sound depends on the breed, so a newborn Chihuahua can whine, but a bigger pup, such as an Irish Setter, already yelps at just a day old.

One very important reflex is that when their neck is gripped, young pups go limp in a foetal position.
This makes it easy for the mother to move pups. But four to five days after birth this changes, and on being picked up the pups' limbs flex as they become stronger.

By the end of the week the Retriever pups' feet have become covered with a light coat of hair.
They now have a silky down on their faces. Their paw pads and nose have taken up a darker pigmentation, and their faces have toned down to a more normal skin pink.

Week 2
Neonatal Phase

Vocalization develops rapidly.
By 10 days Chihuahua pups can yelp, and by 14 days they can bark, while an Irish Setter pup barks by 10 days.

The mother stays close beside pups for most of the first two weeks.
Their sleep time in the first couple of weeks is frequently punctuated by twitching. The mother induces the pups to defecate and urinate by triggering a reflex when she licks their rear end; she consumes the excreta. This corresponds to the period in wolf development when the young stay with the alpha-female in the den, often excavated under tree roots, and consumption of excreta reduces disease risk and avoids attracting predators.

Pups' eyes generally begin to open at about 10 days.
This varies with different breeds: 95 per cent of Cocker Spaniels' or Beagles' eyes have opened by 14 days, around 33 per cent of Shelties', and only a little over 10 per cent of Fox Terriers'. Of the two-week-old Golden Retriever pups of the litter pictured, only one had an eye beginning to open.

Pigmentation continues to develop on the muzzle and feet. The nose is now fully dark.

The coat is noticeably growing.

Head normally still flopped on to the ground for much of the time.

Week 3
Transitional Period

This important week has been called the Transitional Period from the Neonatal phase of the first two weeks into the Socialization Period of greater mobility and play.

For the first time pups usually manage to stand with their tummy off the ground for a short time.
Our pups frequently stood at their front end, but not the back; they made progress with legs out trying to walk. They playfully grabbed littermates' ears, most of the time while still lying down!

Much of the time is spent sleeping and suckling.
When they suckle the pups' back legs still commonly trail flat behind them. They can crawl around backwards as well as forwards.

The pups can now hold their heads out (not fully up).

Eyes now open and respond to light; ears have opened, and pups respond to startling sounds.

Pups move much more, and can fall out of the nest more readily.
They will give a distress yelp to gain attention on being away from the den.

Small bits of meat are now readily accepted, alongside mother's milk.

With this changing diet, their dam no longer has to stimulate elimination in the pups by licking their rears.

With increased mobility, defecation occurs outside the nest.

Social signals between the pups begin.
Pups wag their tails and make little growls – these are not aggressive at this stage.

Pups relate to people more readily.
When held up they may lick your face.

1

2

3

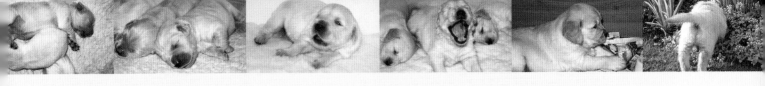

This is the beginning of what is known as the Socialization Period, which runs until around the end of the tenth week.

During this period the nervous system is developing.
Spinal cord nerves develop myelin sheathing. The pups' neurosensory development enables the beginning of play behaviour.

Tail wagging becomes a feature, as does raising the front paw.
Breed has a strong effect on timing: in litters of Cocker Spaniels early waggers begin in the third week, with slow ones starting in their sixth week and the mid-number in the fourth week. However, in the case of Basenjis, while tail wagging started at the end of the fourth week, the late ones did not start until the thirteenth week, the average starting in week six.

During weeks 5 and 6, the pups' teeth show through.
The pups normally gain more access to solid food, and the female increasingly denies pups full access to her milk.

With play behaviour, play barking normally begins between the fourth and the seventh weeks.
As they spend more time in exploratory investigations and social play, the pups spend proportionally less time on feeding and sleeping.

If you extend a finger, they will happily 'suckle' on it.

When pups give a big yawn their new teeth are clearly visible but not all fully through. By this time the pups really have undergone a big change and are commonly about out of the nest.
They are confident of standing on all fours, and spend much more time interested in people. They can also walk about, but are not fully confident.
Our pups are now mouthing and pawing their littermates as their play becomes more active and complex.

The fifth week may be the key sensitive period in the pup's grasp of social relationships.
Part of this change is the beginning of 'pounce' and 'shake' (involved in prey killing), and a sexual element such as play mounting and thrusting.

The pups are still developing, with faces that are still relatively puppy-rounded but their eyes are now much more open.

The pups are now heartily eating solids, but they will still suckle from the mother.
The process of pups continuing to suckle keeps the milk flow from drying up. In the fourth and fifth weeks, as the pups' teeth develop, the dam often becomes understandably less inclined to feed them with milk; and if the pups have eaten solids, they are generally not so demonstrative at the teat.
Many breeders encourage the end of suckling at six weeks to allow a period of at least a week before the pups go to a new home, with the aim of reducing anxiety at the separation; however, left with natural access, the milk will not dry up until the seventh to tenth week.

The dam may regurgitate her own meal, which pups will devour.
This is part of the normal response to demonstrative pups at this stage. This is the ancestral way that female dogs and wolves have weaned and brought solid but broken up food for the pups to feed on.

Play is more interactive.
Play ranges from 'attacking' shoelaces to licking each other more often during games. They also interact with objects, such as ripping and chewing up paper.

The **Retriever pups** have continued to gain size, and their hair is noticeably increasing in length. Their greater strength and mobility is reflected in activities such as standing on their hind legs with their front paws resting on something.

The pups are now very active.
If they are allowed out into a garden with their mother and owner, they will delightedly investigate a wealth of new experiences. With tails wagging, they trot and tumble about with each other, interact with their mother and owner, and dive into the flower border and chew plants.

They are now much bigger, and are still rapidly gaining weight.
They still have that undeniable round puppy shape and endearing nature.

Play

Dogs are social animals, and play is a significant part of their development. Pups need the social interactions of play, especially up to the age of eight weeks, when weaning has normally occurred and the pups are no longer as keen on novel stimuli. While play is important, as pups become older it is important for them to learn our status and play on our terms.

Play has a real ontogeny, or behavioural development. As a pup goes through the transitional period of the third week, play begins, then in the socialization period he develops further in the fourth week, signalling play requests by raising his front paw to littermates. This request capability increases to include the 'play bow', where the pup lowers his chest to the ground and nearly flattens his front legs to the ground; the head is angled up in an entreaty, the tail can beat, and the pup may bark. He may come forwards and then retreat, and repeat these moves to encourage you to join in.

Puppy littermates play together during their development, and so learn the appropriateness of their actions – if they go too far, there are likely to be consequences.

When we play with young pups, the socialization helps them gain a confidence with our species. However, as pups develop and want to play more interactive games with us, they soon recognize that while they can play 'tug' with other pups, they cannot do this with adult dogs; if we play in that way with them we are establishing in their eyes that we are a competitive juvenile, particularly if we are keen to play, rather than an adult. If they pull toys away from us, this further demotes our status relative to them in their eyes. This is training in problems for the future. Certainly avoid your dog 'mouthing' your hand 'in play', as doing so confirms his higher status.

Play should be part of the training of your dog, so ball games emerge from retrieve training. 'Hide and seek' can be great fun for your dog and you, but only when you initiate and command the game.

Similarly, pups enjoy playing with balls or other throw toys, and of course we view it as endearing when they approach us with one. Most of us will want to relate, as we are being 'asked to play'. However, if we do, the pup gains the upper position, whereas we should be the ones that instigate play.

Golden Retriever pups

Black Labrador

Nip it in the bud

One feature of pups' play is nipping and biting, by which they learn what is appropriate behaviour with their littermates. If you allow such nipping, your pup does not know that this is not acceptable: if you get nipped, just stop playing.

A re-run of canid domestication of a fox reveals that domestication itself has produced a more playful animal than its wild ancestor. So too the puppies of early dogs would have gained an extended socialisation period, a longer puppyhood with more time to play and get used to us!

So attracted by the reward of food, less wary wolves domesticated *themselves*, which genetically modified their puppy development times, making some more pup-like in shape and behaviour as adults - and they became playful dogs!

Domesticated
Silver Fox
Vulpes vulpes

SELECTING FOR TAMENESS AND PLAYFULNESS

It was always assumed that humans selected dogs for puppy-like, less threatening features, but events over the the last 50 years have suggested other possibilities. Since 1959 Russian geneticists have bred only from Silver Foxes that seemed 'tamer' and less wary of humans. Each generation has become 'docile and eager to please', approaching humans playfully, wagging tails, whimpering and licking – the foxes have been minimally handled, to avoid habituation, so the change has been primarily genetic (see pages 24 and 33).

With this tamer disposition have come changes consistent with domestication: coat patterns have changed, floppy ears (unknown in wild canids) appeared, rolled tails have also come, and skull changes are seen, with smaller brain cases, underbites and overbites. These changes were not chosen, but have come about with selection for tameness.

One important factor is not to shower toys on our dogs to show that we love them. When a dog has continual access to toys, it becomes much harder to establish that we are the 'pack leader' and the dominant animal; it also reduces each toy's individual signifance for the dog, making it less of a reward mediated through us, the owners. For these reasons it is sensible to put all dog toys away after a controlled games session; this way, the dog comes to recognize that they are your toys and he can play with them when you allow him to.

Play is more common in young than in adults, and carnivores, including dogs, are among the most playful of animals. Play practises the moves of hunting and fighting in an exaggerated way. What keeps play as play, with only inhibited bites, is that initially pups are only gaining co-ordination. But from the fourth week on, even with increasing social activity, their puppy-round faces and floppy ears do not signify real threats. Even when dogs are adults, we enjoy their exuberant play and select for more pup-like, less agressive behaviour.

Sensitive periods

Learning is about getting ready for adult life, and the puppy goes through sensitive periods during development, which are key periods of learning. While dogs can learn skills later in life, there is a correct window of time in which they are programmed to assimilate information at the appropriate stage of development.

Springer Spaniels

The puppy develops from restricted senses, enough for initial suckling with the mother, into a littermate in his own small pack, where he socializes playfully. It is during this period that young pups should be socialized and habituated to people, beginning at 2–3 weeks, and particularly important for the young pack, around weaning at 6–8 weeks. If pups are not actively handled during this period they will remain more fearful of people, which can give rise to fear-biting.

Another sensitive period begins at around the fifth week, when hunting moves, including 'pounce' and 'shake', appear in the play interactions of pups in the litter. Pups under 10 weeks of age make moves to try to pin prey down by landing with their front legs (an echo of the fox pounce).

The Transitional period, as defined by Scott and Fuller, is perhaps the most dramatic week in a pup's life. It starts with his eyes opening, and finishes with his ears becoming responsive to sound. This does not fit exactly into one week, for different breeds operate at slightly different timetables. In this week there is a sudden boost in alpha brain waves, but they do not reach an adult-like pattern until 8 weeks. As a result of these developments, pups are able to move more, begin social communication with littermates and respond to us.

The next big stage is the Socialization period, where the greater increase in developing neurology coincides with greater body development, and the co-ordination of these brings on the sensitive period most identified with forming social relationships, and therefore learning from that, with littermates, parents and others.

Consequently, when we use the Socialization sensitive period of up to 12 weeks to socialize our pups to other dogs and to us, our involvement is taking advantage of the biological system to fully incorporate people into our pup's pack. To show how powerful this time is, when pups are brought up in this period purely with kittens, in later life they relate to cats and not dogs. Scott and Fuller rated the primary socialization window to be the third to the twelfth week following birth; after 12 weeks a growing caution and fearfulness of novel experiences slows the fast-track nature of the period.

Socialization

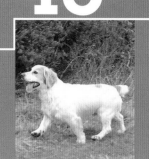

A dog that has not been socialized to people and our way of life is not a liability; indeed, he is exactly as he should be to survive as a feral or wild animal that is wary of people. However, for dogs to feel at ease with our species and relate to us properly and safely, socializing is essential.

Whippet & German Shepherd pup

A dog that has not been properly socialized even to other dogs (pups and adults) can be a most ill-at-ease and unhappy animal. A pup that was isolated from littermates during the Socializing sensitive period will not have fully learnt the appropriateness of some behaviours, and may have a probability of biting, being disproportionately fearful of those around him. Lack of socialization will also make walking your dog a problem.

Habituation to other people is a must if you are to avoid problems with visitors. Do this gently in easy steps, with a new person sitting in a non-threatening position for introductions. Socializing your pup to children is particularly important – however, this is a two-way street, so give children proper coaching beforehand to stay calm, stroke gently and be sensible.

Once you have taken your pup from his littermates you take on the responsibility that, once vaccinated, he can meet other pups. One of the best ways to achieve this is to go with your pup to puppy socialization classes at least weekly. This will allow your pup to meet with similar-age pups and learn the appropriateness of behaviour with other dogs in a safe place. As the inhibition moves change as the pup develops, he does need to know to limit his bites and to learn the balance of proper social deference submission indications.

HABITUATION

- At home, gradually introduce your pup to the existence of home appliances, initially one at a time and at a distance.

- Habituation to car travel is important, to avoid travelling problems later.

- When you start to walk your pup, introduce him first to a quiet road, where he can get used to an occasional vehicle, and give him a treat. Then build up his tolerance in stages.

- When your dog graduates from puppy classes, continue with dog-training classes for further invaluable socializing.

German Shepherd, Springer Spaniel, Long-haired Dachshunds

44

Choosing the sex

When considering getting a dog, one of the single most important considerations, after which breed, is which sex to choose. Intriguingly, what makes a dog male is a 20-fold increase of testosterone in its brain around the period of birth and for the pup's first three weeks. The level then returns to the same as female pups until puberty development.

Springer Spaniel pups

A study by researchers Benjamin and Lynette Hart found that while there was not a noticeable difference between male or female regarding excessive barking or excitability, there was some tendency for male dogs to defend their territories more, and for being destructive, and snappy towards children. Male dogs are also more likely to be wanderers.

Other characteristics normally seen in the male include lifting (or cocking) a leg to urinate, particularly to repeatedly mark upright objects. Territorial urine marking, which can cause problems in the house, is almost always a problem of dominant male dogs. In addition, males are most likely to mount visitors or other dogs, and to investigate women visitors by direct sniffing.

A few studies have shown different responses towards handlers – while female dogs don't appear to show any particular preference, it seems that male dogs may go to female handlers more responsively than they do to men.

Although only a minority of dog owners take their dogs to seek advice for behaviour problems, it is more likely that these will be male: in annual reviews from 1994 to 2003, the Association of Pet Behaviour Counsellors found 58–64 per cent of referred cases to be male dogs.

In general there is a strong tendency for males to be the ones to exhibit dominance towards their owners and aggression towards other dogs. In contrast, females are both more readily housebroken and do better at obedience training than males of the same breed. This division follows the pattern that could be anticipated from the male dog's role in the hierarchical structure of their ancestor's packs.

PARTICULAR BREEDS

If you are considering a breed where aggressiveness is minimal, such as Golden Retrievers or Basset Hounds, these differences are not usually very noticeable at all, so it makes little difference whether male or female is chosen. However, in dogs where aggressiveness can be a particular issue, such as Miniature Schnauzers, or even of moderate aggression, such as Poodles, the disparity between the male and female is generally much more noticeable; in consequence the females of such breeds are easier to live with, with less aggressive tendencies and a consequent greater ease in training.

The period from the pup's 10th week onwards until it reaches sexual maturity has been classified as the Juvenile Period. As the pups get older, and even though the basic behaviour pattern essentially doesn't dramatically change, there are motor skills improvements with a combination of muscle development and practising their use. Pups also gradually learn the appropriateness of particular behaviour to particular occasions.

By the age of 12 weeks pups have begun to become real explorers. At the same time, their distress vocal calls have noticeably reduced, a combination that has a survival advantage. It is during this juvenile period that the distinctive male cocking of the leg to urinate emerges, although there is a big difference between individuals as to when this happens first. This development is partly genetic, but also depends on individual circumstances: as this style of urination is associated with scent marking in adults, rank can have an effect, and cocking of the leg can appear later in lower-ranked dogs.

The onset of puberty varies with both the breed and the sex of the dog. Males of around 4 months begin to become interested in females on heat, but a full intromission that could lead to a fertile mating only starts at about 7 to 8 months. Before a bitch's first season she will show no particular interest in male dogs in any sexual way; however, once she comes into season, males become attracted to her, and she then shows a responsive interest in them. From day 10 of her first season a mating can occur as she has become receptive.

Black Labrador pup

German Shepherd pups

HOMING PUPS

It has been found that pups homed at 12 weeks are subsequently much easier to train than those that are homed at 14 weeks. Nonetheless, despite being neurologically well developed, 'teenager' pups have difficulty in being trained to complex tasks, for as they are very excitable and into everything, they have a corresponding short attention span. (They are teenagers!) However, it is important to ensure that passive training occurs, in that you play with your pup and introduce him to other people with you present. This will improve his capacity to solve problems and to learn new things more easily in training in later life. It is also good to try to ensure that the youngster does not encounter too many frightening occasions, for phobias can begin to develop at this early time.

Generally, it is more commonly advised that homing should be done by 8 weeks, on the grounds that if the pup has spent most time playing with litter mates and other dogs and less time with people, he will not respond as well to people in his adult life.

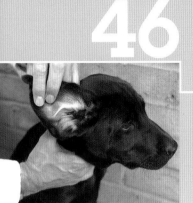

46 Puppy illness can affect adult behaviour

Just as the 'child is father of the man', so the 'puppy is father of the dog'. The importance of what happens to the pup on its subsequent behavioural development is increasingly understood, but the impact of what happens during illness or veterinary attention has been largely overlooked.

Why should this happen?

In a study by veterinarian Andrew Jago from a sample of over 500 dogs, which found that 13 per cent had been ill at some point under 16 weeks old, the most remarkable find was that a statistically significant link was revealed between being ill as a pup and growing up with certain adult behaviour problems: dominance-type aggression, aggression towards strangers, and showing more fear of strangers and of children. In addition, the dogs were more likely to display separation barking and inappropriate sexual behaviour.

Jago concluded that the fearfulness of strangers and children was due to lack of proper early socialization, whilst the dominance aggression, separation barking and sexual behaviour were due to exclusive care and attention producing an overly 'human-socialized' dog. There may also be a link between the date of first vaccination after eight weeks and some behavioural problems.

It is very hard to make direct causal links, for many events happen in the narrow window of puppyhood, not the least being transference away from the maternal group to a new home; even transportation can be very stressful for some pups, as it is probably the first time they have encountered car travel. However, the link to illness as a factor in later behavioural problems is strong enough for owners to make it a consideration at the same time as medical needs.

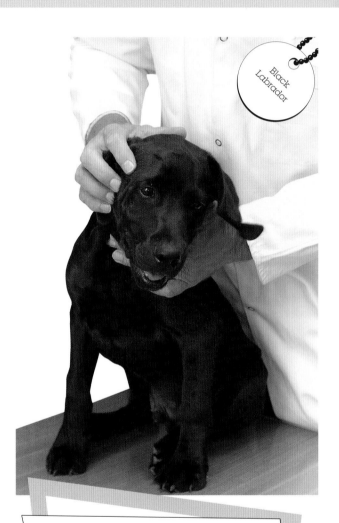

Black Labrador

PUPS AND HEALTH

Ask if there has been medical intervention with any of the pups before making your 'adoption' choice.
Continuing isolation at the veterinarians reduces socialization time.
If your pup becomes ill, make family visits to the veterinary clinic or ask the veterinary nurses to spend some time each day with the pup.
When the pup is home, ensure that it meets a range of people in non-threatening situations. Obviously this will depend on the seriousness of the illness and there may be situations when complete calm is called for. For this reason it may be inappropriate for your dog to meet any other dog during its recovery, which will reduce its familiarity with other dogs.
Remember, however, that your pet's health and appropriate care must be the prime consideration at all times, and it is best to proceed slowly rather than too quickly.

Treating a pup
At a time of the relationship forming between the owner and the pup, regular treatments at the vet's surgery or pills having to be given by the owner can be distressing for the dog. However, with care owners can reduce the effect in older pups by habituation, and pharmaceutical companies are actively trying to make medicines more palatable or, as with flea controls, applied in a dab-on, non-distressing fashion.

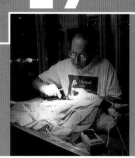

It seems that the number of dogs neutered has been increasing. The UK's APBC (Association of Pet Behavioural Counsellors) found that in 1994, 40 per cent of dogs (males) were castrated and 47 per cent of bitches (females) were spayed; these percentages have steadily grown so that in 2003, 64 per cent of males and 71 per cent of females were neutered. (In contrast, in 2003 97 per cent of both sexes of cat were neutered.)

Why neuter? On a healthy dog, the operation needs serious consideration. A show dog often has to be 'intact' or 'entire' (unneutered), but if you are certain that you are not going to show or breed your dog then it can be appropriate to discuss it with your vet.

A number of behaviours that are sex hormone-related in male dogs can usually be more controlled in neutered animals; unfortunately, neutering can also increase the problem of dominance in dominant bitches.

Although at face value castration should have a simple cause-and-effect linkage with testosterone-linked behaviour, nonetheless it is often not that straightforward. Some vets and animal welfare societies have proposed earlier castration as responsible population control. The outcome for behaviour is unclear: while some studies have shown that there is little difference in aggression, barking or other specific traits, but early castration might make excitability worse, a study by Lieberman suggested that castration at 6–12 weeks might reduce aggression and sexual behaviour.

When carried out at the normal age (usually spaying and castration are carried out on six-month-old puppies), castration seems to have its strongest reduction in inter-male aggression, marking with urine, mounting and roaming – even if castration does not eliminate the problem, it has been found to cut down its frequency and severity. Castration may not 'cure' aggression, but can make such behaviour easier to control.

FEWER UNWANTED DOGS

Neutering is the surgical removal of the reproductive organs to prevent a dog producing unwanted offspring. In some parts of the world neutering is called 'de-sexing', while in other regions the term is used purely to refer to the castration or removal of testes from male dogs; 'spaying' is used to describe the removal of the ovary and uterus from female dogs.

The experience of the San Francisco SPCA has shown how an active, high-volume neuter clinic can reduce pet overpopulation in a city. When it opened in 1976 the clinic was one of the first low-cost neutering centres in the USA, and as a result of its operations the number of dogs and cats abandoned to shelters in San Francisco has dropped by over half in the 20 years from 1985 to 2005.

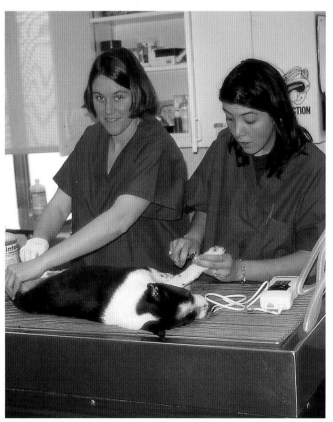

48 Housetraining

Housetraining is all about your anticipating your dog's need to eliminate, and not about your attempting any punishment after any fouling. Housetraining should be co-ordinated with the natural development pattern of the puppy's eliminative behaviour.

Looking for signs

Don't tell off your puppy when he fouls (however irritated by the mess you become), unless you catch it in the act – it will be counterproductive and make the dog wary of you. At three months a pup will want to eliminate every three hours, so look for behavioural signs: the pup will start to circle and closely sniff the ground before eliminating.

Cavalier King Charles Spaniel

Young pups do not foul their nest, as their mother triggers their elimination and cleans it up. When weaning approaches and the mother stops cleaning their body waste, the pups continue her good work of keeping the nest clean. From 7–8 weeks they develop a preference for certain surfaces for use, and at around 8 weeks they normally transfer to a particular site at a distance from the nest.

It makes little sense to train a pup to relieve himself on newspapers in the house, and then retrain him to use the garden. If possible, try to get the pup to eliminate outside in the garden – it is a great benefit when travelling, visiting, showing or in public areas if your dog can be instructed to eliminate at certain times.

Some dogs quickly take to toilet training like a duck to water, assisted by your constant supervision and moving the pup to his appropriate elimination area when you anticipate the need, while others are a bit more intransigent. In this case your two best assets are a clock and a crate (see page 84).

During the period of this training your pup's 'nest' is the interior of the crate with his bedding, and he will hang on to avoid soiling that. Part of this area-restrictive training period is dependent upon your not leaving the puppy in it too long, hence the value of an alarm clock or personal bleeper to remind you it is necessary to take the pup outside at no longer than two-hourly intervals. To avoid 'accidents' en route to the door, distract the pup with encouraging words for the outside, or have a toy in your hand.

When you reach the appropriate area in the garden and the pup begins to eliminate, praise his good behaviour, ensuring that you use a distinct phrase such as 'go now' – if you use this each time, the pup will quickly come to associate it with when you want him to relieve himself. The praise can be supplemented by a good titbit or play.

If you have problems with your dog eliminating at some point in the night, these can often be solved by moving his feeding time to early morning.

Basic training

There is a core of basic training that every puppy should undertake to ensure that not only does he become well behaved and not a danger to you or himself, but that he gains respect for you and has a means of communication with you, which should reduce behaviour problems. An adult dog that has not been previously trained should be introduced to the same core of basic training.

Black Labrador

You should use the same basic training if you are having problems with dominance issues or a specific behaviour problem or problems, even though you will also be attending to specific modifying actions.

To have basic control of your dog, you should be able to get him to 'sit', 'stay', 'come' (or recall), 'lie down' (or drop) and walk to 'heel'. When you begin these with your inexperienced pup or dog, they should take place with a light training lead and an appropriate collar. You can gently begin to do some short training exercises in an area free from distractions in your home when your dog is around 10 weeks old, but don't overtire him, as this is the period when you are also actively socializing him. Don't attempt to do too many exercises in one session.

TRAINING WITH TREATS

Reward training using treats has become the standard method, replacing the choke chain used previously.

Food treats are effective if your dog is keen to respond to food, so training before eating makes sense. Small cubes of chicken have an advantage over dry foods in that your dog won't need to wash them down. Have an easily accessible plastic bag containing the treats in your pocket out of sight, but take out the number you anticipate needing for a simple exercise beforehand: 20 or so cubes are quite sufficient for a session.

Many owners and trainers prefer to guide with and give the treat from the left hand, but the right hand may be preferred in the lead-free style of training. Food held in the hand can help conditioning.

As your dog becomes more familiar with your expectations, you will be able to spread out food treats to be less regular, and use praise as the most frequent reward. Once an exercise is well known, give food titbits only occasionally.

Some manufacturers produce titbits specifically for use as treats or rewards when training; these may be fine for your dog, but food that is already a favourite with your dog is likely to have just as good an effect.

You are pack leader

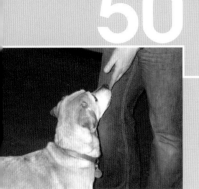

As you are larger than your dog, and stand vertically above him, you start with an advantage as pack leader. You are also in a position to reward and thus reinforce what we recognize as good behaviour – this does not just mean food treats, but also the use of favoured toys and reassuring contact. Any reward or discipline to be effective needs to occur immediately following the event.

assertive. In a vacillating and hesitating owner a dominant dog will not see a clear leader, and he will see it as his role to lead instead.

In an era of fractured relationships and therefore fractured confidence, a woman may feel the need to take on a big dog to protect her home at a time when she may be feeling emotionally bruised. The recipe is the same: the dog becomes dominant, and therefore unsafe. In both these cases, all too often a 'problem dog' is created and all too often euthanazed for our failure.

Labrador

Unfortunately, the majority of owners do not train their dogs in any formal or concerted way; and when they do attend dog-training classes, this is usually only for a short period. Classes in themselves can be helpful, but are not essential – what is more important is that owners understand what they are trying to achieve, implement training properly and, most essentially, portray a clear image to their dog of a benevolent leader.

It is this last point that can cause problems. In the modern world it can be hard for many people to know quite how they should behave: in the 'man's world' before the mid-20th century, when men were regarded as 'providers', men are thought to have been more matter-of-fact and direct with dogs. How much men have changed may be debatable, but it is clear that many now have difficulty in being firm and

In control

You should be the dominant one in your relationship with your dog, but 'dominant' should not be mistaken for 'domineering'. You need to be a firm but benevolent leader, not a despot, as being the latter can exacerbate problems with very dominant or wary dogs.

Any communication from you to your dog, whether by short, clear vocal commands, body language or signals, or a clicker, should be clear and unambiguous. It is essential that *you* initiate events such as feeding or going for walks, rather than on the demand of the dog, or you will find that he tries to usurp your senior position in the relationship.

Springer Spaniel

'Passive dominance', demonstrated in such actions as not allowing a dog to go through a door first, not feeding him first or allowing him to pull on a lead, is equally important. Your body language, from open welcoming to a dominant stern stance, needs to be clear, and in this you are being an actor who has to convey a message, rather than allowing your emotions to get the better of you.

Distance commands may have to be quite exciting and encouraging. In such a situation your clear visual body language of going away and not towards your dog will evoke most response as his 'pack' is moving off. For outdoor work you should use specific hand signals that relate to spoken commands, but don't get self-conscious or tone down your signs, body movements or calls because you think you will look silly – remember that uncontrolled dogs can cause accidents and be dangerous.

Part of your communication system will be rewards. The dog needs to know that only good behaviour is rewarded: don't confuse your command system by ad hoc treating. Once your dog does what you command, then reward him immediately – timing is very important here.

The better trained your dog becomes, the more that his reward can be praise rather than a food treat. Your dog is happy when he can understand and act on what you convey,

for it is a two-way communication, and the dog gains a clear and reassuring understanding of your relationship with him.

Turning your back to withdraw attention from your dog needs to be done cleanly and definitely: dogs are clever, but they are able to do better if we convey our intention in an understandable and unambiguous way. Your dog is evaluating you all the time, and if you slump on your sofa with him on your lap, allow him to eat off your plate or snap at people, you are giving him lots of information – most of it bad.

CONFIDENT CONTROL

- Give clear commands to allow your dog to know you are in confident control.
- Don't attempt to bully your dog, as this can be counterproductive.
- Be firm and calm, but also analyse what is going on and how your dog is behaving, and attempt to see just how clear your instructions and behaviour are to him.
- Words like 'sit' are short and sharp and clearly different from our normal delivery of 'walkies', and dogs understand the difference.
- Ensure that the clearest thing you are conveying is 'I'm in charge, so everything's OK'.

52 Using the lead and collar

The lead is the single most important piece of equipment involved in training, as it allows you control over your dog. For larger breeds, even well trained ones, it is appropriate to have a strong lead; don't buy a short lead, as a standard walking and training leash should be long enough to keep your dog close or at proper walking distance. An adjustable three-in-one training leash with three length alternatives can be useful.

Puppies should have an appropriate-sized collar that is soft and wide enough to span across two vertebrae. As the pup grows, the collar will need to be changed – normally you should be able to put two or three fingers under the collar: any less is too restrictive, but any looser and the collar could catch and pull off. Similarly, puppies' leads should not be too heavy. For most adult dogs a straightforward collar that buckles up and has a lead attachment point is appropriate.

While check chains and submission collars can be an asset when appropriately used, and today there is rightly far more caution over their use than a few years ago, they should only be for training purposes and should be used as a quick check and release of pressure. The chain from the ring should be worn so it passes around the front of the dog's neck, with the loop running round the neck to pass through the chain ring on the side of the dog nearest the handler; the dog should be on the handler's left-hand side. The weight of the chain keeps it loose around the dog's neck, apart from when it is used to check. Avoid using a choke chain on young pups or other dogs with vulnerable necks, and never use one as a constant restriction with a dog pulling continuously on it – this is a complete failure of function, and can be damaging.

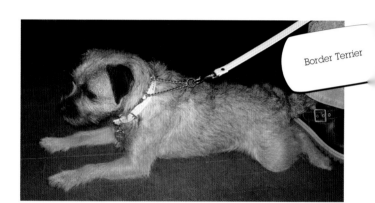

Border Terrier

A better form of choke chain, which brings control with less risk to the dog, is the half-check collar, where the half made of chain lies over to the back of the dog's neck but the front half that crosses the windpipe is made of fabric. But while these chains can be helpful in the training of boisterous individuals, it should still be remembered that any check collar can be potentially harmful to the windpipe: walking a dog should not be a matter of being pulled, and proper training and proper control should overcome this.

Head halters and harnesses can be used in particular circumstances. Over recent years a range of head halters, where the halter fits over the dog's muzzle as well as round the neck, have come on to the market. If the dog pulls, his own movement causes him to bring his head down, which counters the pulling action. Other halters swing the dog's head back towards the owner, again reducing the ability to pull.

Many owners like to use a body harness, as this puts no restriction on the dog's breathing, and any restraint is made on the whole body. However, a harness does require the dog to have been properly taught to walk appropriately beside his owner, and that he does not suddenly pull, as this is potentially dangerous for a frail owner.

It may seem strange at first, but much early training of a pup about the house should be on a lead, as this acclimatizes the pup to the use of the lead and collar.

Lhasa Apso

EARLY LEADS AND COLLARS

It seems that dogs have worn collars as long as people have owned and trained dogs, and collars can be seen in early pictures and other images, such as those portrayed on the ancient Egyptian 11th-dynasty Pharaoh Antef II's stele (memorial stone), made some 2,000 years BCE.

A number of historic dog collars have survived, some made of heavy leather, others brass ones with hinges, locks and the initial letters of the owner's name, with a coat of arms for the nobility. Dogs being controlled with leads attached to collars are also shown in early images of large mastiffs pulling on leads from the palace of Ashurbanipal at the Assyrian city of Nineveh (645BCE); even earlier images are seen on the mural relief in the Mustaba of the Egyptian Old Kingdom 5th-dynasty court vizier Ptah-hotep (below), showing long-legged Basenji-type dogs with collars being used to hunt Scimitar-horned Oryx and other prey.

Cocker Spaniel

Extendable leads

Retractable leads on sprung spools give great flexibility and a degree of freedom and control, but ensure you use the correct weight lead for the size of your dog. The lock enables the lead to be worked as a fixed-length line.

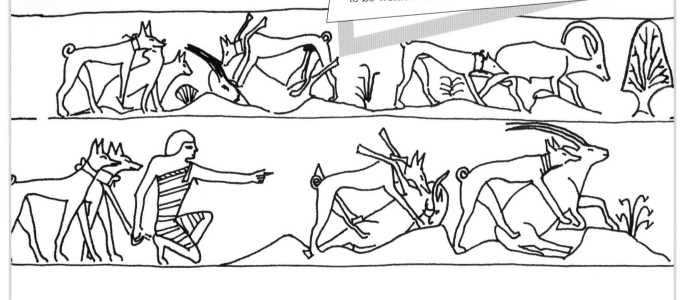

53 Crate care

If a crate has been provided for a dog from puppyhood, it is a place of reassurance, not of confinement. Crates are not for punishment, but are a useful training tool, and have the added advantage of offering safety when travelling by car. As a training tool, the crate is invaluable with pups who don't readily take to housetraining, and can make a playpen for the pup.

However, the crate method is not infallible, especially if dogs are left in it for too long while housetraining, or if a crate is too large compared to the dog. Abuse of proper crate management carries real risks for a young dog. The nature of the adult dog depends upon good socialization, and isolation can give rise to emotional disturbance. Dogs should not be shut away for long periods, for they may become stressed, which will lead to behaviour problems; in some cases, dogs can show signs of distress when released into new, unrestricted circumstances, even their own house. Unfortunately this causes some owners to think 'he loves his crate', rather than realizing that their excessive treatment has led to agoraphobia.

Dogs are social animals, and positive attention is necessary for their well-being and balanced behaviour. For this reason, not only is time limitation essential for crate training, but it should also be coupled with exercise and interaction when the dog is out.

Sealyham Terrier

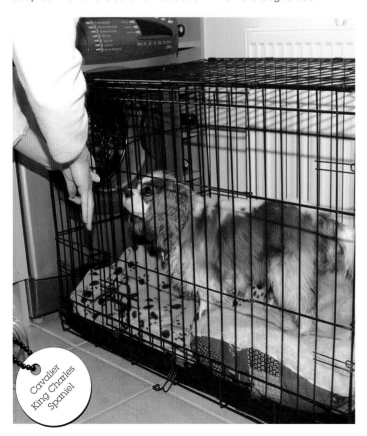

Cavalier King Charles Spaniel

CRATE TRAINING

Before you can use the crate for housetraining or care, it is important that your pup is properly introduced to it to establish its role as a den. Ensure that you locate the pen in the house where you won't fall over it or bump into it, but preferably in a place where you are nearby, such as a corner of your kitchen or bedroom at night – dogs generally prefer to be crate-confined in an area where their owners are about.

Keep the crate's door open, and put in your pup's bedding, water in a bowl that he won't tip over, and a toy. Then encourage your pet into the open crate with titbits and a clear phrase that you will use each time to encourage him to enter, such as 'into crate'. In most cases puppies readily take to having a crate as a 'base', and will go in of their own accord.

When your pup has been happily going in and out, shut the door of the crate, and soon the pup should be snoozing. However, once you start using the crate, remember your responsibilities to your pup, and ensure you exercise him before and after putting him into the crate, and don't keep him in the crate for longer than two hours.

'Sit' is one of the most important commands of basic training. Sitting is a useful position to place your dog in when you wish him to calmly withdraw from another, less desirable activity; and for road safety it is invaluable to sit before crossing, to allow time to consider when to cross and to be seen to be in control.

White Siberian Husky

The traditional way to teach 'sit' is to have your dog positioned on a leash to your left. By keeping the leash held above the dog with the right hand, and using a gentle downward pressure on his hindquarters, saying 'sit' as you do so, certainly works.

Using today's reward system, have your dog come to you, standing in front of you. Then, with a small food reward in your right hand which the dog looks at, flex your wrist up, raising your arm over his head. This will naturally cause him to sit down. As he begins to sit, say 'sit'. Then praise him, and follow that with the titbit. If you have a problem, it could be that you have your dog too far away from you, so as his eyes follow your hand he does not tip back – with small toy dogs, don't leave your hand too high or they will end up dancing on their hind legs!

When you have repeated this a number of times successfully (and you will probably be delighted how quickly your dog picks this up), then move to position yourself so your dog is on your left side. Using your right hand, hold a treat in front of his nose, then sweep your hand back over his head, curling your wrist up as you do. Again say 'sit' as the dog begins to sit, reward verbally and give the treat.

If you are using clicker training (see Way 87 p.122), either wait for your dog to sit by chance, or engineer this. As he stands in front of you, again move a treat to make him sit and click exactly on the point of sitting, then treat him. Repeat this a few times. Note that with clicker training, you have said nothing so far, no commands and no praise. The next time you do this, say 'sit' before moving your hand up with the treat, and repeat a few more times.

Mongrel

'Stay'

'Stay' is a necessary development of 'sit'. For your dog's own safety, there will be times you want him to be positioned for a period, not the least on the vet's table, and this command is also useful for general control, especially when you have visitors. However, do not leave your dog in this position for too long – remember when you have said it!

German Shepherd

If your dog moves too readily on a slack lead, careful use of the lead as a vertical stay at arm's length may help him to understand the initial requirement. Develop the activity by extending the lead a little more at a time. After a few sessions with the lead on, place it down and repeat the exercise without holding it.

If you want to use the clicker method, (see Way 87 p.122), this is also a development of 'sit', but it becomes 'stay' by extending the time after your dog sits until you click and treat. Build up in simple stages: say 'sit' and wait five seconds before clicking and treating, then next time ten seconds, and keep increasing the time to a minute or so. If you anticipate that your dog is about to get up, click and reward to ensure that the command is reinforced.

Border Collie

Pyrenean Mountain Dog x St Bernard

Nervous dogs

For dogs that have separation problems, which can include rescue dogs from shelters, you should be aware that this command may be hard for the dog to deal with. As a result, spend more time repeating the exercise close to the dog than you might with a less anxious dog.

Now that your dog has learnt to sit and stay, the next most important basic training exercise is to ensure that he will come to you on command (also known as 'recall'). In many situations this will be the most essential exercise for your dog to know, as he can be recalled safely if danger threatens when he is off the lead.

Black Labrador pup

Right from when you obtained your dog you will have been using his name in appropriate times, so he should know the word means him; in this exercise you use his name automatically.

With your dog on a long training lead, tell him to sit and stay, then walk away some 3m (10ft). Turn, then allow a food treat to be seen and call out your dog's name in an encouraging tone, followed by the instruction 'come'. Some people prefer to put a hand down towards the ground to proffer the treat, and to make this move the subsequent hand signal for recalling the dog; others prefer to open their hands welcomingly as a signal, and even to squat down to emphasize this. Whatever you do, be consistent. Repeat the process.

As your dog arrives, it is recognized good practice to command 'sit'. If you have progressed to standing when calling 'come' and have a food reward in your hand which you keep against your body at waist height, as your dog looks up to it he will often sit automatically. It is safer and more controlled for the dog to sit obediently after coming to you.

When you move to take the lead off, make sure to consistently recall your dog; it is advisable to undertake this training initially within an enclosed environment without distractions. As with other basic training exercises, begin to cut down the treat reinforcing as your dog becomes consistent. Because you should sound encouraging, this can be the most fun of the exercises for both you and your dog.

If using the clicker method, (see Way 87 p.122), stand with your hand down low holding out a treat, and say your dog's name. As he starts to move to you, click and treat directly. Repeat, standing a little further back. After a few times with no other words, use the command 'come' after his name.

Training the growing dog 87

57 'Down'

Because your dog will be more relaxed lying down than sitting, he is likely to be happier to stay in this position for longer periods with you, initially in the home and then elsewhere.

Cavalier King Charles Spaniel

Get your dog to adopt the 'sit' position on your left. Then swing your right hand, holding a treat on the underside, down in front of your dog, bending your knees and back at the same time until your right hand is about 30cm (12in) from the ground. (If you have neck, back or knee problems, you may find starting in a kneeling position easier.)

As the dog goes down, following your hand, say 'down'. When he has adopted the lying down position, give him the food treat as a reinforcing reward. When he does the exercise well, stand him in front of you and repeat as before.

To use the clicker technique (see page 122), hold a food treat in the same way under your right hand and lower it down towards the ground in front of your dog. When he has gone fully down, click and put the treat down in front of his head between his paws. (Leaving the treat avoids the problem of his trying to follow your hand up.) Once he has repeated this procedure a few times, introduce the word 'down' as you lower your hand; repeat a few more times.

Vulnerable dogs

Some dogs may find that such lying down exercises make them feel vulnerable, but immediate reward should soon reassure them Do not feel tempted to manually pressure your dog into the 'down' position, as if he is a dominant animal doing so could unsettle him.

Pyrenean Mountain Dog x St. Bernard

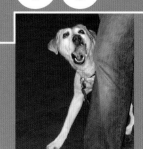

Training to walk to heel is a key need for a safe dog. Just because your dog shouldn't go out and about until he has had a full course of inoculations (usually by 12 weeks), this doesn't mean you can't walk him on a lead: you can encourage a pup to walk to heel initially in your home, and then in the garden.

There is no absolute right or wrong way to begin this important training. Some trainers believe it is better to train to walk to heel after learning to sit, and some before; again, some think it is far better that a dog learn to walk to heel without a lead first, while others prefer that it learns to walk to heel with a lead in the first place.

As all these systems are initially done inside and the reward is a food titbit, each works: the learning system on reward works very well, but what is key is that you use the commands 'walk' as you set off, and 'heel'. (A reinforcing hand signal in front of the dog's face on 'heel' can help.)

For training in the house and garden a soft collar should be appropriate: acclimatize the pup to wearing the collar on its own for relatively short periods, then wander about the house with him on a light loose lead to allow him to get used to its feel.

When he is completely relaxed, you can move to controlled heel walking. Your lead should be held in the right hand, and the lead should run loosely across your front to your pup, with your left hand able to lightly hold the lead loose. Get your dog to sit, face him, allowing him to know you have a treat in your left hand, then position yourself on his right, keeping your left hand near your waist.

As you step forwards on your left foot, say clearly 'walk' as you move forwards; your pup will naturally wish to move with you. With careful positioning of the treat hand, his natural desire to move forwards ahead will be diverted.

Some trainers prefer to gently check forward movement by holding the collar while saying 'heel'; others prefer the entire procedure to be controlled by the titbit reward. To turn, move the hand with the treat in the required direction – the dog should follow. Saying 'steady' to anticipate turns is useful.

Some pups respond best to a toy in the left hand. The lead is normally anchored in the right hand, as most people are right-handed and if a dog pulls, he is held by the stronger arm.

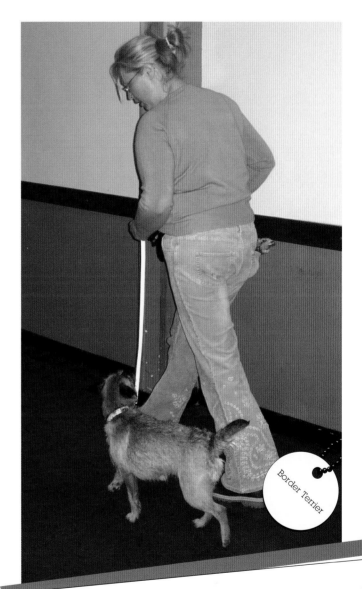

Border Terrier

Training pups

Remember only to do training with a pup for brief periods at a time, as he will tire. At no point scold the pup, but use reward and encouragement to get good results. Don't try to train your pup if he is bored, as tired or bored pups may just flop out and you will have got nowhere with the training.

5

Dealing with problems

Cavalier King
Charles Spaniel
(CKC Spaniel)

Avoiding behaviour problems

Owners of dogs, like parents, have a responsibility for their charges' proper guidance and training, and unless a proper plan of action is thought out and followed through, chaos will ensue! Owners owe this duty of care to the other members of their family as much as to their dog.

Cavalier King Charles Spaniel (CKC Spaniel)

Many behaviour problems arise from inappropriate behaviour by owners, because of a lack of understanding of the dog's viewpoint. Fundamentally, most 'bad behaviour' is really behaviour that we consider inappropriate in our own lives, yet it is normal canine behaviour. What we consider destructive behaviour is standard behaviour for a dog: quite reasonably from a dog's perspective, if he can chew bones and toys, why should he not chew other things about the house? It is up to the owner to make the distinction.

Dominance and aggression

Children are often bitten by dogs because the owner has left a group of small, boisterous children alone with a dog; with the dominant person gone, the dog may not perceive himself to be a lower rank than small children in the 'pack', and he can be competitively stimulated, particularly by ball games. When owners take their dogs on walks in neutral territory where other dogs are met, such as a park, the potentially most risky encounter is between same-sex same-size animals. The owner's reaction at such times is critical: straining on the dog's leash can dramatically increase the probability of aggression or even a fight.

The single biggest error that runs as a thread through most dog problems that owners encounter arises from failure to address the issue of dominance. All too often, owners of small dogs think they don't need to be trained, 'because they can't do any harm'. Aggressive small dogs can be just as disruptive to a household as big ones, and when one partner insists on treating the dog as 'my baby', this is seen to be justification for spoiling it and not fulfilling its needs. Biting and aggressive dogs, large or small, can be a real danger; in most developed countries the law recognizes this, and such dogs will be destroyed.

Problems in the home

It is not always the case that a problem dog has not been 'trained'; it has, by default – but to do all the wrong things. When we acknowledge that our dog has a bad habit, or more usually a package of bad behaviours, we should look at ourselves first, as the chances are that we have caused the problem in the first place or made it worse.

Many people are entirely delusional about what they believe to be the state of their relationship with their dog. In homes across much of the developed world, family relationships are in turmoil and lives are made a misery due to the appalling behaviour or aggression of the household dog or dogs. As a consequence family members take sides, arguments develop, causing additional problems between partners and between children and parents, such as some family members colluding with the dog's keenness to take food by slipping him bits from their plates while they are eating their own meal.

Owners may not see the extent of their problems, but visitors certainly do, especially when they are asked by their hosts as they arrive, 'You do like dogs, don't you?' Visitors' safety and peace of mind can be put at risk when large dogs barge them aside or jump up when they arrive and nearly knock them over; the same dog may later try to mate with the poor visitor's leg. Alternatively, the guest cannot sit beside the host on the sofa as a small dog is already there, barking loudly – or perhaps they cannot sit on a particular chair because 'That's the dog's favourite'!

Life does not have to be like this: a home without appropriate consideration for its dog and human companions is not a pleasurable one for the dog – let alone the people. Remember that for many centuries, only Toy dogs were pets in the modern sense – working dogs did not have full access to the household – and act appropriately in your dealings with your dog.

Boxer

The role of the owner

Boxer

NO PARKING BEYOND THIS POINT

Shar Pei

Pet behaviourist Roger Mugford has made the point that blaming owners can give rise to feelings of 'guilt and failure'. He is right, dogs can have behavioural problems for a host of reasons, and not the least of contributing factors are sex (males have more dominance problems), breed, breed lines, source of dog and, one of the most significant, whether the dog was properly socialized as a pup. There are also many veterinary reasons for behavioural problems. Even if we have not caused the problem, we can help improve matters.

We must appreciate that our dogs are communicating with us all the time. If a dog has picked up information leading to bad habits or making them worse, by changing our approach the dog can also change; this is not only good for ourselves and our family relationships, but also for the survival chances of the dog. Unfortunately, we all know owners of problem dogs who apparently accept that their dog is 'just like that' rather than believing that they can change the situation.

Owners are the ones who can really turn around their dog's lives. By looking at the relevant problem page and referring to relevant information in other parts of the book, I hope you will be able to develop a programme to improve your dog's behaviour and your relationship with your dog. Improvement can happen whether or not your dog has a behaviour problem, for we should never forget that huge numbers of dogs live great lives happily with their owners and are not problems!

In this section of the book you will find information relating to specific problems with targeted advice. But if your dog has one problem, it can often have a few, and consequently a basic package to reduce the risk of problems should be to:
• Be a benign but firm leader
• Exercise your dog regularly for the appropriate amount
• Practise basic training exercises
The Solutions on page 101, for example, are not only appropriate for the problem of aggression, but will help in the overall relationship.

If you cannot crack a problem by yourself, sessions with a dog trainer can be of great help, or you can consult a professional dog behaviourist. In the UK, look for organizations such as the British Institute of Professional Dog Trainers, the Association of Pet Behaviour Counsellors or the Canine and Feline Behaviour Association; in the USA, the Association of Pet Dog Trainers, the International Association of Animal Behavior Consultants or their equivalents can advise you of one in your area.

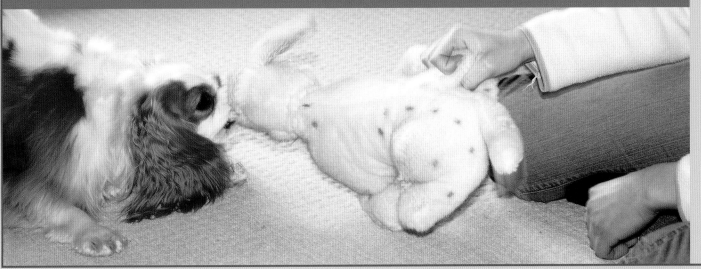

59 Pulling on the lead

This is one of the most common problems, and shows a fundamental lack of control. If you have an adult dog that pulls, do not despair, as you are not alone – go out on any walk, and at least a third of all dogs on leads that you will see are straining ahead of their owners.

Shar Pei

Pulling on the lead is often a sign that your dog is dominant in character, although it can also arise from insufficient exercise and too much confinement; the dog's delight in being out causes him to want to race on. A dog pulling when walking can make it such an unpleasant experience for owners, particularly if they have bad backs or bad necks, that they may give up trying or just not walk out so often.

In this situation, it's back to basics through the whole gamut of training, reinforcing that it is you who is really the top dog. Particularly repeat the training exercises of 'heel', using the same recipe for walking an adult dog as for training a pup. The single most powerful technique for stopping an adult established puller from pulling is to turn abruptly and go back in the opposite direction. Praise your dog if he is at a better pace, as he initially will be. If he then begins to pull again, just repeat and repeat. Within a matter of minutes most pullers will realize that as you are dictating the direction, you are in charge, and he will have to walk more at your pace.

WHAT NOT TO DO

The last thing you should do is struggle, pulling back against the dog on walk after walk, with him making semi-strangled sounds as his windpipe is restricted, as this reinforces a dominant dog's belief that he is the leader. In the same way that pulling back against a dog when he sees another can make it more likely that a fight will follow, pulling back against the dog inevitably makes him want to pull forwards when walking. So don't do it, as it just increases or even causes the problem.

Owners may have endured for years being dragged along pavements, trying to keep their feet. When a professional dog trainer takes over their dog, and in a matter of just a few minutes transforms him into one that walks properly, they are amazed. Not all dog training and behaviour correction takes long; many things can be achieved in a short time.

Shar Pei

Grabbing and tugging the lead

When you begin to introduce your dog to that vital piece of equipment, the lead, it may seem like a great toy – he may grab hold of the lead, pull it about, chew it or start a pulling game. This may just be high spirits, but if permitted to continue it can destroy any programme of training.

A lead made of thick rope is a clear sign that the owner feels the need to have it strong enough to counter the dog pulling, and even thick enough that it can't be bitten through; it is a clear indication that the owner has abdicated control to the dog – the lead has become a tug-of-war toy, and the dog has won a higher rank of dominance than is safe.

Specially designed tug-of-war toys should not be used with dominant dogs, as the owner can 'lose' in the dog's eyes. The lead should never be used in this way, as a dog that is regularly able to grab, tug or chew its lead when wearing it is very unlikely to walk properly on a lead without pulling. This has hierarchical implications for yourself and your family, and teaching your dog appropriate leash manners and behaviour is one of the basic needs. Some breeds are more likely to tug or chew the lead; in a study carried out by Scott and Fuller in the USA, Basenjis were most likely, while Whire-haired Fox Terriers and Cocker Spaniels were most accepting of the lead.

SOLUTIONS

Spray the lead with a bitter-tasting proprietary spray.
Sprays can be obtained from your vet or some pet stores.

Go back to the basic training of 'sit' (see page 85) and walking on a lead.
It may even be necessary to go back to starting indoors to minimize the distractions of the outside world.

If the dog grabs the lead, say 'No' firmly then instruct the dog to 'Sit'. Allow the dog to sit quietly for 30 seconds, more if necessary, then give a reward.
Begin walking to heel on the lead; as you step forwards, it is most likely that so will the dog. Praise good behaviour and carry a toy or treat to distract him from grabbing the lead.

Go through exercises on retrieving objects
Repeating this trains the dog that you are in control. When it picks up the thrown object cal 'come' and on its return say 'give' and reward release.

Ensure that you give the passive dominance signals to your dog that you are in charge.
As the pack leader you go through the door first, not him; similarly, you go first on stairs; your dog is not allowed to sleep on your bed, or be up on your furniture, and so on. Ensure your dog is trained and respects these signs.

You can use the head halter as a tool in training or retraining.
The head halter is not a muzzle; however, a gentle pull on the leash has the effect of closing the dog's mouth and pulling his head downwards.

Airedale x Alsatian

Meet the mother
There is a significant genetic component in responsiveness to leads, and a study carried out in the USA showed that in cross-breeds the first-generation pups were found to behave in a similar manner to the mother.

Not coming when called

Before leaving the park, you need to put your dog back on to the lead. You call, but he refuses to return. You feel foolish, your exasperation shows in the irate tone in your voice, and so you try to catch the dog, only for him to run further away; and when you do catch him your dissatisfaction shows only too clearly as you tell him off – a catalogue of errors!

You underestimate your dog if you think he can't anticipate that the off-lead time is coming to an end as you move towards the gate and as this is the only time you call to him! As part of a regular walk you should do some training exercises, which include calling your dog to return. Try to avoid putting him on the lead at the same approach point and, most important of all, do not tell him off when he does return or as you are putting him back on the lead – this forms a bad association in his mind, decreases his keenness to return and is entirely counterproductive.

You certainly should not chase after your dog, for he will run about more, thinking it is a competitive game. Yet how often do we see owners starting to run after their dogs, trying to catch them, as a regular part of a walk, oblivious to the fact that they have created a bad training pattern that reinforces bad behaviour. If he is unsure of your ranking in your pack relative to him, this behaviour on your part will merely underline that for the dog. Male dominant dogs are most likely to pay less heed to training, so your role is most significant. Remember, your dog is a pack animal: as you walk away, he will want to follow.

If you have one of your dog's favourite toys in a bag or pocket, you have a specific dog-magnet, and you can use this to play with your dog for a period. Do not use it just as a lure and then pounce with the lead; instead, genuinely spend time playing and reward the dog with praise once you have made him sit. Only then put on the lead. Once your dog appreciates that returning when you call is rewarded rather than 'punished', he will want to comply.

The reality of a dog not returning when called is a clear indication that *your* behaviour, rather than his behaviour, is giving the wrong signals. It also shows that you must really spend time with basic training (see page 79), especially the 'come' exercises both indoors and outdoors. If you are using an extending lead to ensure that the dog does not run off during the exercise, at no point should using it become a 'tug-of-war' or hauling the dog towards you, merely a quick check to his movement.

One thing that makes a dog less interested in returning to you is other dogs; this is where attending training classes and practising recall commands among other dogs has such value. You can then work on recalling your dog in open spaces among calm dogs on their owners' leads.

Pyrenean Mountain Dog x St. Bernard

Be exciting
The further away the dog, the more you need to project your call and use large visual signals. Make calls high-pitched, repetitive notes, or use a whistle, as well as his name and 'come' or 'here', and make them encouraging. While walking away may work, so may running around waving your arms and then lying down, still waving – what dog could resist being curious? As he gets better, you can be less flamboyant!

Coming home to a dog-trashed room or a destroyed lawn can be annoying, but the key issues are commonly those of separation anxiety. However, a significant component can be just boredom. Try to discover if your dog is anxious when alone. A clue is that anxiety is involved when there is more than one problem, so digging may be linked to fouling, for example.

If a regular increase in exercise is coupled with an increase in obedience training, this gives a better level of interest for your dog and reinforces your proper role. It also increases a dog's feeling of security to realize you are in charge.

Grey Wolf

SOLUTIONS

- Create a place in the garden where the dog can ease anxiety tension and gain enjoyment from digging.

- Create a dog sandpit where he can dig, and initially reward him repeatedly with a bone in the preferred hole.

- Hide treats deeper when your dog becomes used to his 'digging spot'.

- To passively discourage your dog from using former digging areas in your absence, block them for a period. (To reduce the probability of your dog returning to old dug holes, when you return home from a walk with your dog's droppings in a 'poop-bag', drop them into the bottom of the hole, then cover. Your dog is unlikely to re-dig.)

- In hot areas, dogs may dig to create a cool, shady pit. To counter this, ensure that there are plenty of cool, shady areas in the garden, plus an adequate supply of water.

- A dog is less likely to dig after eating, so shift his timetable and feed him in the morning rather than in the evening.

Anything can be chewed

Destruction may not happen from anxiety or even boredom, but because you have trained the dog to think anything can be chewed. This happens when in a misguided attempt to be kind, owners buy and supply their dog with large numbers of toys. Keep toys to three at any one time.

As with digging, the cause of chewing the arms of a leather sofa is likely to be separation anxiety, but boredom itself can be a key factor. Leave a dog alone with an insignificant amount of exercise, and it's a recipe for destruction; a 1994 study found that puppies left alone for hours on end were likely to show destructive behaviour when left alone as adults.

While digging to bury the odd bone is one thing, repetitive digging from boredom and frustration can ruin a garden. Separation anxiety can be a key issue, and dogs re-homed from animal refuges have a higher probability of being insecure and are likely to dig when left alone.

Golden Retrievers

Separation anxiety

Left alone at home, a dog that feels insecure may howl or bark to gain contact. This lack of security is often more marked in dogs that were not properly socialized with people when young. This can be a real annoyance to neighbours, and is not pleasant for the dog, so try not to leave him alone for long periods on a regular basis.

CKC Spaniel

The separation anxiety suffered by a dog can not only be annoying for neighbours; if it manifests as destructiveness, it can become a version of hell for the owners – some owners come back to a destroyed leather sofa or apparently trashed rooms. It is all too easy to be annoyed and to punish the dog, but that really won't help, not least because it is after the event. The reality is that the dog has been distressed and that he's caused the problem to the owner because of this, so the dog's distress must be addressed.

As with a number of problematic behaviours that are stress linked, separation anxiety is susceptible to gradual habituation. It is essential that the owner's leaving of the house is not made into a drama. Too many of us have insufficient time when going to work or to a meeting, and so the household tension can rise. Think what this does for the dog as he gets swept up with the tension, building to a dramatic departure. Before we can control our dogs, we must control ourselves. A peaceful departure becomes less of an issue for the dog.

The habituation itself is to break the concern over departure and time, to reduce the significance of departure, and to do this in easy stages. Allow the dog to see you leave, but return after a minute or so. Repeat it many times, increasing as you do the time of your 'absence'. It is as critical that you do not make a fuss of your dog on your return – ignore him, and allow a later low-key greeting after you have had him sitting for a period. All this diffuses the tension and makes your coming and going less of an event, and consequently it ceases to be emotionally charged for your dog.

SOLUTIONS

- Reassure your dog with your scent rubbed from your hands on to a favourite toy. Treats such as a marrowbone presented before you leave can also be a focus for attention.

- Leave owner-scented clothing or cloth in the dog's bed to bring contact reassurance.

- Some dogs respond to interesting food in a toy, which diverts them for a good period.

- Don't make a 'goodbye scene' with your dog; depart quietly, unseen.

- During the transition adjusting period, shut your dog away from where you put on your coat and make other signals of departure. Do these out of sight, and then just go.

- The peak time for anxiety is around half an hour after the owner's departure; when gradually habituating your dog to your departure, this is the most critical period.

German Shepherd

There is not just one type of barking, and problem barking tends to come in a linked behaviour package. If someone is skulking by the window of your house, you will be pleased that your dog goes into watchdog barking mode. However, if the person is just walking past on the pavement, you will be less happy if your dog keeps up a persistent barrage of barking.

In general, excessive barking within the home (other than in watchdog mode) is linked to an active, excitable, demanding temperament; such dogs also tend to snap at children. The Miniature Schnauzer fits this profile, and although this is a playful breed, dominance towards owners is a big issue. By contrast, the Golden Retriever is less prone to excessive barking in the family home even in a watchdog role – and significantly, the breed does not have dominance issues with owners.

When approaching the problem, evaluate the needs for your household and check whether your relative dominance or lack of it in your dog's eyes is an issue: if you have a dog snapping and barking at you, preventing you from sitting on your own sofa, you have a dominance problem!

Mongrel

German Shepherd

SOLUTIONS

• Acknowledge your dog's alertness, then allow him to see that he has done his job and you have taken charge by instructing him to sit beside you.

• With excitable breeds, the subsequent instruction to go to his bed distracts the dog from the original repeat behaviour. Remember to praise him.

• If the barking is purely to gain attention, turn aside from your dog until he stops barking. Reward him only when he has ceased to bark for a little while. An interceptive sound or other distraction can be helpful.

• Don't shout at your dog – he will think you are just joining in, especially if he is a terrier.

Barking on command

One of the best ways to bring both calm and your authority properly into your dog's eyes is to train him to bark on command, using the operant approach. When your dog barks, use the command 'speak', and open and close your hand like a dog's open mouth above his head. Reinforce with a treat reward. Try to anticipate barking, and repeat the sequence. Use similar reinforcing to end the barking.

For the safety of the dog's owner, family and other people – and for legal reasons – it is vital to control aggression. Problems with aggression are the cause of many young dogs being euthanazed, so it is vital that owners can prevent the dangers of aggression.

If your dog growls when you go to move toys, food or the dog from a chair, he is showing dominance by possessive aggression, and these are key situations when a dog is likely to show aggression to his owner.

It must be clear in the dog's mind that you, and not he, are the pack leader. In numerous ways you should regularly assert your top role – regular training across the range of general training exercises asserts this.

SOLUTIONS

- It is essential that the dog is trained to walk properly at heel and does not pull on the lead, as pulling shows he has taken the dominant position.
- Proper control to prevent your dog barging through doors ahead of you shows you are dominant.
- Regularly grooming your dog asserts your position.
- When aggression is being shown, tell the dog to lie down, which makes him lower and thus in a more subservient position.
- When appropriate with a suitable-sized dog, lifting him off his front legs removes the dog's autonomy (similar to the longer-term effect of grooming).

It is usually not a good idea to be aggressive back to a very aggressive dog: first, if he is behaving out of fear, he may bite (see page 103); second, if he is acting possessively, he may bite (see page 108); and third, if he is very dominant towards you, he may bite. Turn away, ignoring the dog, allow or encourage the situation to calm, then systematically tackle the problem, as described above. If your dog is being aggressive towards you, others are also at risk, and you should also implement the solutions opposite. If you have further concerns, seek professional help from a dog trainer, pet behaviourist or vet – not all problems are safely resolvable, but most can be.

Very dominant dogs are often not affectionate and become less controllable on becoming adult. Most bites from such

dogs occur when owners try to punish them and the dogs react to their authority being challenged. When the owner backs off, this reinforces the dog's belief of his status, so try to avoid such a confrontation arising.

The strategy of ignoring the dog, withdrawing your affection and following the solutions points normally causes the dog to work out that he gains reward by deferring to you – you have passively elevated your status. Use a 1.2m training leash and a collar in the home to restrain aggressive and dominant behaviour, and reward your dog when he obeys you.

German Shepherd

If your dog was not properly habituated to people when a pup, he will naturally want to defend his pack and territory from strangers – this is perfectly normal behaviour for a pack animal. However, if you ever wish to see any visitors or receive mail, this needs to be overcome.

In a controlled manner, set up a 'visit', with the dog on a lead and a 'visitor' already in the room, seated to be less of a threat and armed with a normal training reward of food or a toy. The visitor should not show any fear, and should start by ignoring the dog and conversing in a relaxed manner with you, the owner, not looking at the dog. If a visitor can stay at your house for a few days, the dog becomes used to 'strangers', but visitors need to understand that they are assisting a training programme. This will need to be regularly repeated, or you may end up leading a monastic life!

In extreme cases of aggression, evaluate your situation and determine whether you need direct professional help from a trainer or behaviourist. In male dogs castration may be advisable.

60–85 per cent of attacks against people are in the dog's own home, against family, friends and neighbours.

SOLUTIONS

- Everyone in the family should eat before the dog does.
- Do not give snacks under the table or off a plate.
- Train your dog to eat only on command.
- Do not allow your dog on to the bed or couch.
- Train your dog to walk to heel properly, to sit on command, and to be properly in your control over basic commands.
- Walk your dog regularly.
- Your dog should not be first out of the door, but last.
- Do not allow your dog to bully anyone for attention; everyone in the family and visitors should understand that this is stopped by not rewarding him – do not be interactive until the dog stops, then get him to sit, and reward good behaviour.
- Groom any potentially dominant dog daily.
- Do not play tug-of-war games over toys with dominant dogs.
- Do not leave young children alone with dominant, aggressive dogs.

Dogs and mail

People delivering mail should not be intimidated by dogs, and owners should not leave dogs in a front yard or garden if there is any risk, or put the post box at the exterior of the property. If your letterbox drops mail on to the floor and your dog destroys it, put a mesh box on the back of the door so the dog cannot get at the mail. If the 'culprit' is a small dog that grabs the mail as it arrives, the problem is usually excitement, often linked to barking. Break the habit by setting up a phony mail delivery with a friend, and distract the dog each time a letter is dropped preferably by voice. Or get your dog to sit some distance from the door and reward, then repeat with a letter dropped in; and if your dog stays, reward him. By ensuring the dog is calm, with this desensitization by habituation he will learn to ignore letters.

Boxer & Staffordshire Bull Terrier

When you go for a walk with a dominant dog or a dog that was not socialized to other dogs when he was a youngster, every dog appearing on the horizon can make you anxious. Your dog will probably bark aggressively at other dogs, and may even attack them.

Do not anxiously pull on your dog's lead: pulling back increases the dog's aggressive intent, and is exactly what fighting dog handlers did to enrage their dogs before releasing them. In addition, pulling doesn't just have this effect for one particular meeting – by doing this on different occasions, you are actually training your dog to strain at the lead to challenge other dogs. He may even end up making the association that going out on a lead means being ready to fight.

Familiarize yourself with your dog's body language so that you can read tail and ear signals to anticipate his behaviour when you see another dog in front. If your dog stiffens with an intensity and a fixed stare at another dog, his focus has already moved his blood adrenalin levels a few notches higher. If your dog's head is diverted away, eye contact is broken and the situation can be diffused. Head halters that pull to the side are very useful for this purpose, and you can also use your dog's favourite toy to distract him.

Once you have your dog's attention, command him to 'sit' and then reward him. The great advantage of 'sit' is that it takes your dog into a world where he knows that you are in charge and all is safe.

SOLUTIONS

Repeat basic training in a park, using a long line to ensure attention, particularly working on 'come'. Then ask a friend with another dog to walk towards you on a distant parallel line. Stay relaxed and in control of the situation, and focus your dog's attention on a treat or toy in your left hand before he becomes alert; you can also turn his path with a turn halter. When he ignores the other dog, reward him. Repeat this training a number of times, gradually getting less distant until you are able to repeatedly walk past other dogs with no problems.

Border Collie & Mongrel

Muzzles

Most owners don't want to put a muzzle on their dog as it seems to demonstrate a failure of control and state 'I've got a dangerous dog'. However, others, even though it is safe, will keep their dogs well away and thus reduce confrontation! A muzzle can also keep your dog from being bitten while you train him to behave differently.

Patterdale Terrier & Weimaraner

Fearfulness and phobias are commonly encountered problems. If dogs are brought up without being socialized to people, other dogs and strange objects, they will be naturally wary: fear and wariness are the normal state of an unsocialized adult dog, and to train such a dog to be relaxed and happy with people and other dogs involves some effort.

Some breeds and breed lines produce animals that genetically start as fearful or phobic. Certain small breeds are particularly prone to nervousness, and Collies can have inherited a fearfulness tendency to noise.

Breeders and new owners need to be mindful that at around the age of 8–10 weeks, in the socialization sensitive period, pups may have a greater reaction to frightening events, which can leave them phobic; a bad experience at this time can leave them emotionally more cautious.

Boxer

Many people live with a fearful and wary adult dog and are conscious that they need to be reassuring and give support, as it is important not to frighten fearful and phobic dogs. Do not punish a fearful dog – this will only increase his fearfulness. The dog may give mixed messages, indicative of its internal concerns: he may run up, wanting to approach, but then show ambivalent behaviour in shying away from hands or handling.

With phobias in adult dogs the most reliable behaviour approach is that of gradual habituation (also known as desensitization), which can be supported by conditioning. In habituation the approach to the object of the phobia is undertaken slowly and incrementally as the dog adjusts. In classic (Pavlovian) conditioning the object of the phobia is associated with rewards, from affection to food; however, once the phobic object goes so to does the reward, so an association is formed that the previously phobic object equals good things!

PHOBIA OF OBJECTS

With dogs fearful of washing machines, vacuum cleaners or pushchairs, for example, follow the approach of not making the behaviour worse by over-reacting or by comforting him; instead, behave normally. Keep a dog fearful of strange objects on a lead when out and about. Gradually take your dog closer to the feared object, but do not walk directly to it; approach it tangentially and stop at the mid-point, looking away. Rewarding with food treats is particularly effective. In stages, over some days, go closer.

CKC Spaniel

Noise phobia

Do not become reactive to the noise or too comforting, which will reward the behaviour. Carry on in a friendly manner, as if nothing is happening. At another time with your dog on a lead in a room, play a tape or disc of the offending sounds, initially very quietly, then gradually play the sounds more loudly over days and weeks, keeping your reactions normal. Reward good behaviour with titbits, toys or affection.

Fear of people and dogs

An anxiety caused by nearness to strange people or dogs is most likely to come from lack of socialization when a pup, and can also arise due to isolation for health or other reasons. Such a dog is neither enjoying a happy life, nor is it safe – and is a dangerous animal for a vet to have in his consulting rooms.

CKC Spaniel

A dog that is fearful of people will try to escape confrontation by going behind his owner or under a chair where possible. If he feels threatened and cannot perceive a retreat, he will cower with tail and ears down, and may bare his teeth, growl and snap as a threat. The dog will back up to a wall behind him and feel no option but to bite; in extreme cases, he may defecate or urinate from fear. If this has become an established pattern of behaviour, it may also become self-rewarding as people usually back off and move away, and the dog's fear lessens.

Do not pet and reassure your dog when he carries out fearful behaviour; this reinforces the problem. Do not punish fearful dogs, as this aggravates the fear response.

If a friend or trainer is happy to help, let the dog see the person at a non-threatening distance while you focus your dog on his lead with an instruction to 'sit' and then a reward. Next, get your helper to approach from behind and pass by at a distance without looking at the dog or interacting; if this action does not evoke a reaction, reward again. Eye contact is threatening to the dog so it is essential to minimize this, keeping eye and body looking to a different direction than the dog. It may also be appropriate to have a muzzle on your dog during habituation training, to protect your helper.

When appropriate, after passing from behind, get your helper to stop and kneel down, and to proffer a treat on a flat palm. Walk the dog forwards to take the treat. Repeat a number of times. Over time the helper's body can turn towards the dog, but avoid eye contact at all times. After many repeats the helper can undertake the task standing.

Fear of dogs can be countered in the same way as for aggression towards other dogs, with the co-operation of a helper with a dog, starting at a distance and gradually coming closer.

Be patient

Remember that dogs' problems can be deep-rooted, particularly those caused by fear. Even if your dog responds well to the exercises here, it can be a matter of months before he is able to fully overcome the problem and become confident enought to behave normally, so take your time and don't expect immediate results.

Boxer

Chasing prey by running it down is how your dog's ancestors survived. The chase for food was the most essential prerogative, so the urge to chase moving objects or animals is deeply ingrained in your dog's genetic ancestry.

Unfortunately, the problem may not remain one of chasing, but may escalate to killing livestock such as chickens and lambs. One study looked at 59 cases of livestock predation and found that only 34 per cent involved single dogs – the rest of the cases involved a dog 'pack', and over half the attacks involved a two-dog 'pack'.

If you have your dog as a young pup, socializing him to other species will make him less likely to chase them when adult – farmyard dogs do not chase livestock around, as they have become habituated to them. A gradual habituation in stages to other species, using the crate to contain your dog, can impart a familiarity and lessen the urge to hunt.

The key is to be sure that although your dog is focused in investigation or pursuit, you can distract and recall him. In an area without distractions, put your dog on a long leash to retain control (but not for continuous pulling) and have a toy thrown that he will chase after. Call him back in a very encouraging way, using a favourite toy in your hand that you know is more attractive than the first; if he responds better to small titbits of food, use these as reward. Ensure he is well praised on his return.

When you are sure he and you have mastered this, move to a more 'real' setting and practise there. When this is successful, upgrade the activity to practise 'come' and retrieving exercises at some distance from livestock, still on the long leash until you are certain your dog will return to you despite interesting distractions.

Remember also that sheepdogs of all types have been selected across the centuries as dogs that can both carry out a hunt and be inhibited over killing, following the instructions fo the shepherd. Unfortunately, there are instances when sheepdogs, alone on fells or hills in the absence of the shepherd's control, follow through herding into chasing and killing. This is only goes to reinforce the basic premise that, however well trained they are, dogs should not be allowed to roam alone, particularly where there is any chance of them meeting prey animals.

The chase

However, in some dogs the desire to hunt is naturally so powerful that you may be unable to overcome it alone; in this case do not allow your dog off the lead in farmland or other likely places. Keep up the retraining not just on this exercise but on the basic gamut of exercises, which reinforces his focus on you as leader (see page 80), and seek professional help if you cannot overcome his natural desire to chase. Don't forget that most of his chases will be 'practice' with a strong element of play, but these can easily flip into the real thing with an attack.

Golden Retriever

71 Chasing cats: a breed basis

The sighthounds (Afghan Hounds, Borzois, Deerhounds, Greyhounds) and terriers (Jack Russell Terriers, Yorkshire Terriers, Scottish Terriers, Stafford Bull Terriers, etc) have the worst reputation for pursuing an old enmity too far: they are inveterate cat chasers and, occasionally, killers, and in pack situations they are much worse.

Feral dog & cat, Thailand

It should not come as a surprise that the sighthounds and terriers are most likely to put cats at risk, as they have been selected to pursue and kill. In contrast, sheepdogs, herding dogs and gundogs have been selected for their group hunting skills, but without of the kill. Toy breeds are not selected for activity, and working dogs have specific functions.

With terriers and cats in the house you always need to have caution, but with proper introductions and sufficient care, harmony can be achieved. Not all terriers are as strongly anti-cat as each other, and terrier man Robert Killick believes that, for example, West Highland White Terriers and Norwich Terriers are less persistent than Airedales (top).

Angela Collett of Greyhound Rescue reckons that although many Greyhounds would kill cats, 25–30 per cent can be homed immediately with cats.

Stopping pursuit of cats by the breeds with a bad track record can be hard. However, apart from the need to live alongside other people with their pets, if your dog dashes after a cat across a road, he may become the victim. If you cannot control him using the same techniques as for chasing other animals, seek professional help.

INTRODUCING DOGS AND CATS

A good way of introducing a cat and dog is to first allow them to meet by scent only. If the cat is being introduced, keep your dog out of a room and allow the cat to wander about it. Then take the cat out, and subsequently allow the dog in. Do this a few times so both animals become gradually habituated to the existence of the other. You will also be able to gauge something of your dog's response. On the assumption you have trained your dog to a reasonable level, and he is in your control, then get him to lie down on the floor of the room. Then bring the cat in inside a secure cat carrier (preferably metal) and place this up on a surface, such as a dresser or worktop. Carry on, not making a fuss, and sit down, keeping your dog lying or sitting by command. After a few minutes take the cat in the basket out. Repeat the process, gradually bringing the cat out for longer periods, until they have got used to the presence of each other.

When you do allow them to meet in the first instance, put a muzzle on your dog if he is a terrier, a sighthound or another breed about which you have concerns. Only remove the muzzle when there is a low risk, and ensure that the cat has plenty of vertical retreat places, such as shelves.

Remember that your considerations in making the introduction successful are not just the safety of the cat; cats are readily stressed by threats to their personal territory, and can react by fouling, spraying, aggression, furniture damage or increased roaming. Pups socialised to cats are less risk.

Cats fight back

Unlike the pack-ancestry dog, which has a variety of submissive moves when cornered, solitary cats are well armed and may make ferocious last-ditch defence moves – even a German Shepherd may get a fistful of claws across the muzzle.

Although a bicycle or car may not seem like prey to you, if their movement conveys to your dog the excitement of running after prey, he may be after them like a shot!

Ensure that your dog is safely on a lead in public places and anywhere there may be vehicles, and that you have good control over him – it can be very dangerous for other people's lives as well as your dog's to have one that is 'addicted' to chasing vehicles. If you have already achieved a good level of control over your dog and the basic commands work, especially with the 'come' exercises as outlined on the previous page, the solutions here may solve the problem. However, the instinct may be deeply ingrained in some breeds, and if you find you cannot overcome it by yourself, seek professional help for your specific dog.

Car chasers

Retreating cars stimulate certain breeds, where chase is at their heart, more than others: sighthounds, such as Greyhounds and Whippets, are born chasers; sheep-herding and droving dogs, including the Border Collie, Shetland Sheepdog and Bouvier des Flandres, readily pursue cars; and terriers are great chasers.

Boxer

SOLUTIONS

- Get a friend to cycle at a distance, and walk towards him with your dog on the lead or side-pull halter at a parallel.

- At any sign of change in your dog's interest in the cyclist, turn and walk in the other direction. Then go back again, and repeat and repeat.

- Reward the dog with a treat when he shows no interest.

- Then stand with your dog where your friendly cyclist can go past you, starting from behind you – this is the test, for the vehicle 'running from him' is his trigger.

- Again use the head halter to turn away, then command 'sit'. As he does so, reward, and repeat and repeat.

When two wolves each have an end of a piece of meat, there can be a possessiveness tussle, with threat growls – this is perfectly normal in a wolf pack. However, it is entirely unacceptable and unsafe to have a dog threateningly baring its teeth and growling, or snapping at anyone who tries to pick up a toy or his food bowl. He is clearly demonstrating that he thinks it is his, and this shows that your dog does not regard you as being in charge in your own home.

CKC Spaniel

SOLUTIONS

Toys

• Put a toy (not his favourite) beside the dog. Get him to 'sit', and reward him if he does not have the toy. Repeat.

• If your dog is not particularly threatening but will not readily yield his toy, give the 'sit' command, then offer a treat; as he exchanges it for the toy, say 'give' and praise him. Repeat as necessary.

Food

• Again with the dog on a training lead and someone else checking the lead when necessary, instruct your dog to 'sit'.

• Put down the food bowl containing bland food, and as he goes forwards to eat, distract him with a loud short staccato voice sound. Repeat each time he tries to come forwards.

• When he stays in position, reward him with a treat. Take up the food and repeat. This time, after the reward, when he stays in position say 'Food' or another term that you will only use when you want him to eat.

Chairs

• With the dog on a lead on the chair, put a treat reward in your other hand and lower it until the dog moves forwards for it. Say 'off'. When he is off, get him to 'sit' and reward him.

With some dogs this also occurs over his sleeping area, which he may have decided is one of your chairs. If a visitor tries to sit down on that particular seat, the dog goes into a terrifying possessive threat display. The same can occur with a dog in a car, threatening to protect it violently against anyone near: while owners may think this is no bad thing to deter potential thieves, it is a different proposition when it occurs to family or friends.

To avoid getting into this situation, train your dog from the beginning that you are in control of giving food and toys to him, and remember that some breeds are more dominant than others – terriers can become particularly possessive.

Jumping up

74

Jumping up can be a real problem, especially with large dogs, whose weight can be overwhelming for elderly, frail people and children, and muddy paws on clothes are rarely well received. If jumping up is a long-ingrained habit that you have been unintentionally rewarding, you will need persistence to change it.

For some large dogs of more naturally dominant breeds, jumping up can be a means of asserting themselves, but usually it is what it seems, a greeting. Adult dogs in a group may sniff and lick, but the behaviour is most clearly seen when a mother returns and her pups jump up and lick around her face in excitement. Consequently it is not surprising that this behaviour with humans occurs mainly in pups and younger dogs (6–18 months) when we return home or when visitors arrive.

When the dog is young, most owners get down on their haunches and encourage him to enthusiastically greet them; how unfair it then is when, having 'trained' the pup to do that, we suddenly try to push the dog off and scold him for doing the same when he gets a bit older!

When does the problem occur? Is it when people arrive, when you meet them out on a walk, or when your dog meets children? When you know this you can then focus on practising the substitute behaviour and reward for sitting in those circumstances in a controlled way that you have set up, as shown in solutions, right.

The reality is that we should not view jumping up as bad dog behaviour, just unsafe. Once you can understand how your dog views jumping up, you can make efforts to solve the problem.

SOLUTIONS

- Don't be too enthusiastic as you return home; don't put your arms out in greeting and stay standing. Your aim is not to increase the dog's excitement.
- Don't engage in eye contact and don't behave like a puppy yourself.
- Don't tell your dog off for jumping up when he is pleased to see you, help him to gain pleasure by being rewarded for another activity – sitting. It is not that his behaviour is wrong, just inappropriate for the safety and comfort of people, so rewarding an alternative behaviour is good for your dog, for you and for others. Give a clear verbal command to 'Sit', then when the dog does so, reward him (with praise, appropriate calm stroking, a click or, initially, a small piece of food).
- Don't let other people undermine your efforts. Other people may unwittingly undo your training by their enthusiastic greetings. Make them your conspirators – most people will play along if they are told that they are helping. Just ask them to remain calm and upright, to ignore the dog, and to talk to you while avoiding eye contact with the dog.
- Put your dog into another room while the initial human excitement calms down. If there is a threshold of excitement for your dog that is tipped over by visitors arriving, this can be initially hard to overcome. So if your family, whom you haven't seen for months, is about to arrive, remove the dog from the potentially stimulating atmosphere.

German Shepherd

'Sit!'
All this will fail if your dog does not clearly understand the basic 'Sit' instruction, so you need to work at it. Dog training and avoidance of problems is about doing the work, so repeat, repeat, repeat the basics, but not for long sessions – five minutes at a time is sufficient.

In a survey of 4,000 respondents in the USA, Barry Sinrod found that 47 per cent of dog owners allowed their dogs to sleep in the same room as themselves, and 60 per cent allowed a dog to sleep in their bed with them. When the human partner was away, 66 per cent allowed their dogs to sleep on their bed. And where 13 per cent of partners were unhappy about having a pet in bed with them, the partner ignored their concern.

Some couples get to a point of having next to no sex life or even close contact because one partner insists on having the dog in the bedroom at night. It is not just the more intimidating, larger dogs that growl – even toy breeds can become aggressively defensive when 'their' half of the couple is on the bed and the other attempts even to sit down.

This situation usually arises from one of the partners spoiling the dog – and spoiling the dog means exactly that: treating it as a toy or a plaything, and not treating it fairly as a dog. Indulging small dogs can aggravate dominance problems, which can lead to others in the household being threatened or bitten by the dog; and even large dogs, such as German Shepherds, may threaten, growl or even bite if they believe they are higher in the 'pack order' than the human partner. If the confidence of that person is visibly lessened, the dog becomes more assertive.

Aggression problems with dogs on beds are not limited to partners; children and others can be threatened by the dog,

Mongrel

and when no one is in the bed, some dogs may urinate in a dominant marking manner.

Even when aggression is not a factor, disturbance of sleep can be a big issue. The dog moves around, reducing the comfort of the owner, or the owner responds to the animal scratching to be let out or back in. Almost incredibly, dog behaviourists have encountered extreme cases where, rather than confronting the dog, owners have ended up sleeping on the floor – nothing could more clearly send out signals to the dog that he is top dog!

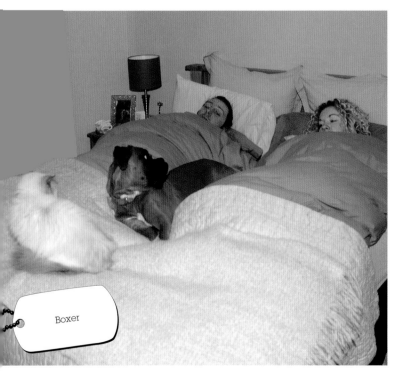

Boxer

SOLUTIONS

▪ A dog receives entirely inappropriate rank position messages by being allowed to sleep with his owner. To support other actions to reduce dominance issues generally (such as not feeding scraps from the table, and the like) and to overcome bedroom aggression in particular, the dog should be barred from the bedroom completely.

▪ Both owners and dogs that are used to co-habiting may take a restless night or two to adjust, but the dog can be reassured by having an unwashed old T-shirt of the owner in the dog bed.

Mounting legs and hypersexual behaviour can seem strange and worrying to owners, not to mention embarrassing when someone's legs are mounted or your dog is attempting to mate with the rug on the floor while you are having a conversation.

Bearded Collie

SOLUTIONS

- Neutering often stops the behaviour.

- Heightened excitement can occur when guests arrive. Use the approaches suggested for submissive urination and separation anxiety to reduce the dog's perception of excitement.

- If excessive play and petting increase a dog's excitement to a threshold, remove him into a 'cooling off' room for a minute or two and allow him to become calmer. Do not leave him for prolonged periods, but bring him back in, instruct him to 'sit' and reward the good behaviour.

- Anticipate the specific approach of the dog by standing up and moving away to reduce his focus, then instruct him to 'sit' and reward him with a treat when he does.

- Distraction techniques, including toys, can help.

- Using a water pistol while stopping the act can help to reinforce the negative association to the dog.

Even when owners are successful at reducing their dog's mounting of family member's limbs, the dog may differentiate between them and visitors, who may suddenly find themselves on the end of his amorous advances. And for young children, a dog the size of a Labrador landing on them, holding them with their front legs and making mating movements, can be very scary.

However, a young male wolf, or young intact male dog in a feral group, will naturally attempt to mate with females of the group, so we should expect the same to happen with unneutered male dogs, usually aged 1–2 years, in our 'pack'. (Females in season occasionally do this.) Mounting can also be a reflection of lack of proper socialization to dogs when young; and in some young animals a component funnelled into repeat sexual activity is pent-up energy due to lack of appropriate exercise.

Owners who have a couple of intact male dogs under 3 years old can be disconcerted to find that the dogs are not only mounting people, but frequently each other. In some situations, such a mounting attempt can have a component of dominance.

Boxer

'Stealing' food

Feeding from the table is not only likely to encourage obesity; more immediately it leads directly to behaviour problems. Unfortunately too many owners view such feeding as a little conspiratorial indulgence between themselves and their pets, without realizing the harm they are causing to their dog and his relationship with them.

Boxer

SOLUTIONS

• Titbits of food in training should be given exclusively to reward good or required behaviour in the dog, when you choose to give them, not to the dog's demand.

• Train your dog to take food when you permit it, and to recognize that food comes via you.

• Do not prepare the dog's food where you eat – do so in your kitchen, not at the dining-room table.

• Assuming that your dog has been trained to obey the command to sit, put his food down in a bowl, but keep him in the sit position, then allow him to eat the food with a simple command used each time, such as 'Eat your food'.

• Don't confuse your dog by giving him end-of-meal scraps on the plate you have just used.

Scavenging was a normal and important part of his ancestor's survival, so taking food does not seem wrong to a dog. If a dog begs for food while you are eating and you give him a bit, that behaviour has been rewarded and you have conditioned the action into a habit – the food acts as a reinforcing reward to the dog. Too many owners try to excuse what they see as their dog's 'bad habits' when a visitor's food is devoured off their plate, or the dog makes family mealtimes a misery by pushing for titbits, or worse, just walks off with the meal! The problem is not the dog's bad habits, it's the owners' bad habits that have caused the situation, and until this is faced, the dog will not change.

This bad habit of many owners also undermines their own standing in the hierarchy in their pet's eyes, for what the owners see as harmless indulgence of their pet is the reverse of the logic of the wolf pack, where the highest ranked animal is fed first and others do not intervene.

While so many problems can occur with dogs because of dominant dogs and unassertive owners, submissive urination is one of the clearest examples of the reverse situation. It is not wrong behaviour, for such submission to a much more dominant or aggressive dog will prevent attack. It is more likely to occur in young dogs and in females than in males.

A typical situation is when a nervous, excitable dog has been anticipating a visitor. The dog recognizes the visitor as dominant from past experience and is at once excited, wagging its tail, keen to greet, but portrays submission by lying down and dribbling urine, displaying extreme submission. The posture can also be adopted when standing or crouching, but it will not be a regular urination pose.

Submissive urination can also become a habit at times of 'set-piece' excitement occasions. In particularly excitable dogs that have a predisposition to this, the looming dominance is far less a factor than the excitement. It can also be the response combined with submissive posture to challenging or demanding situation in the presence of a dominant owner or trainer.

Some dogs are more prone to submissive urination than others, including Cocker Spaniels, Golden Retrievers and certain German Shepherds.

In situations that bring this on, such as the family greeting outlined above, you can anticipate it: keep the excitement at a lower key and make the greeting outside, avoiding fouling the house; alternatively, place the dog beforehand in another room well away from the family greeting. Allow the excitement to occur without the dog, and subsequently allow the dog to meet the visitor in a much lower emotional key. The visitor should be quiet and also ignore the dog at first greeting, and preferably be sitting.

If this occurs in response to your normal arrival home, it is particularly important to make no fuss: do not greet the dog in such a way as to excite him, and be calm and effectively ignore him. Subsequently at a later time, when the dog will have adjusted more calmly to your presence, greet him quietly.

Where he is responding to you one-to-one with submissive urination, lighten your voice encouragingly, lower your height to be less dominating, do not pat or touch the dog, and encouragingly redirect him to rise to a ball or some food in your hand.

SOLUTIONS

- Do not make a fuss about the urination.
- Punishment will entirely reinforce the existing problem.
- Initially only introduce people at a distance well beyond that which makes the dog uncomfortable.
- Rewards make all the difference, especially food rewards.

Where it comes from

Submissive urination seems likely to have its origin in the mother's stimulation of urination by licking her young pups' genitalia; when this happens they remain passive. According to Fox, this behaviour is retained into adult life, so that when dogs meet, the more submissive presents its groin and goes passive as the other investigates – in extreme cases, submissive urination is the final result.

79 Rivalry and pecking order

The introduction of a new dog or puppy into a home must be approached with care. While most owners assume that the existing resident will automatically remain top dog, this doesn't always happen. Wolf pack life is never just about alpha and omega – there is always a bit of relative rank at issue – and in our own pack there may be rivalry if the dog thinks that other members of the family are not of higher rank, as well as the top-dog owner.

To ensure the canine pecking order is maintained, it will be necessary to demonstrate to the resident dog that he is favoured. This will also reduce jealousy in the resident, as he will be in effect rewarded for the presence of the new puppy. Once a clear hierarchy is established for further peaceful co-existence, it is better in dog terms to treat the top dog as the top dog, which then reduces the challenges of the other dog.

The canine world, from the wolf to your dog, is not inhabited by democrats open to discussion, but by committed adherents to hierarchy. In your relationship with dogs, therefore, you need to be sensitive to their needs and acknowledge these by greeting the dominant dog first and allowing the dominant dog to go through doors before the other – but don't politely stand back for them, as they will assume you are a submissive wimp!

SOLUTIONS

▪ Many aggressive interactions, even just spats, are sparked off by a staring match, where the non-dominant dog should look away. Reduce friction at the point of a potential issue, such as feeding time, by ensuring that the dogs are positioned to eat so they are not looking directly at each other.

▪ A dog with a bone still wants the other dog's bone, and this can be a real point of contention in multi-dog households. Giving bones to the dogs in different, separate locations avoids this from becoming an explosive focus.

More than one

In the 2004 National Pet Owners Survey in the USA, over a third of owners had more than one dog, with 23 per cent having two, and 12 per cent having a pack of three or more. Each of these households has a dog pecking order.

Long Haired Dachshund

German Shepherd & Pyrenean Mountain Dog x St Bernard

It is necessary to groom breeds with heavy coats on a regular basis to avoid matting. Some breeds, such as Airedales, need a shaping coat cut and grooming to prevent them looking like yaks in a short space of time. Furthermore most owners assume that grooming is just a matter of appearance, and do not appreciate its significance as part of their relationship with their dog in his behaviour and training.

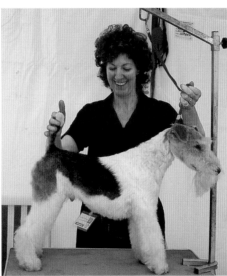

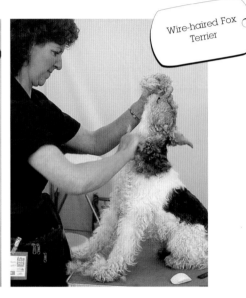

Wire-haired Fox Terrier

Dominant dogs will often rise up to put paws on a lower-rank animal, but do not appreciate it being done to themselves. Dental problems (such as cleaning the teeth), a wedged foreign object that needs investigation, nail clipping, cleaning eyes or putting in eyedrops can be anything from a minor to a serious issue with some animals, even for vets and professional groomers if your dog fights their attentions. However, if you are able to brush your dog's coat on a daily basis, this informs your dog that you are in charge of him, and not the other way round.

With dogs that are not used to grooming and are dominance-contentious, make sure you have fitted a training leash and halter; however, do not undertake this until you have established basic training commands and are sure that your dog responds properly. Initially extend some grooming from stroking, and build this up as the dog accepts it. Do not start on danger areas such as the head, but initially on the back.

At no point become impatient with your dog or fight him into position, for both of you will suffer from the stress and he will be even less keen to co-operate. If you make the whole experience a pleasurable one, he will find it enjoyable and will be happy to repeat it.

As with most types of training, habituating your dog to regular handling, both by yourself and other, should start when he is a puppy.

Matted hair

As dogs have a great knack for getting filthy, it is necessary to be able to groom properly, for putting a dog with a matted coat into a bath will just make a tangled mess if he is not groomed first. If the coat has become stuck together in a knotted mess, it may be less stressful to the dog for a professional to clip and shape it out. Do your homework and consult a professional groomer for the appropriate combs, brushes and other equipment for your dog's coat type. A small dog is easier to groom on a table top, but make sure it has a non-slip surface, and don't leave him unattended.

Fouling the home

Fouling in the home is harder to assess and evaluate in dogs than could be expected from what seems an obvious problem.. When considering fouling in the house, it is important to carefully consider the nature of the fouling to ensure that the correct problem is being tackled.

With cats, fouling the home is not uncommon and is frequently caused by stress from overcrowded conditions. In contrast, while this can be the cause with dogs, researchers Voith and Borchelt found it in only a fifth of all their cases. After aggression, soiling the house has been identified as the most common problem encountered by dog behavioural counsellors; loss of toilet control due to anxiety has been seen in about a third of separation-related behaviour cases in bitches, and about half in males.

If fouling always happens when you are away from the house, even when your absence is relatively short, this has the characteristics of separation anxiety (see page 98). If fouling occurs when you are in the house, it may just be your dog is not fully housetrained, so go back to basics (see page 78). When crate training to aid housetraining is used properly (see page 84) it is usually effective, but if this captivity system is abused and the pup or dog is left too long it entirely undermines the system.

Dogs brought into the home by visitors can trigger a bout of urine marking by the resident dog; and new objects brought into the home, which can include boxes or bags from the supermarket, can be a focus for corrective overmarking by your dog against the unfamiliar smells.

Where your dog has developed a territorial pattern of marking set places in your home, he will be drawn back to them by his scent and will feel the necessity of remarking on top of the scent. It is therefore imperative to clean the site up thoroughly using enzyme proprietary products, as your dog's nose will detect lower scent concentrations than yours.

A significant number of dogs do not eliminate outside in the garden or on walks. Their owners are generally aghast at what they interpret as the perversity of their pet, when in reality the dog may have become fixed on a location or type of substrate in the house, and may not be properly housetrained. It may also be that the dog will not eliminate in the presence of their owner or a family member who may have been overfirm with punishment, so the dog is fearful.

Mongrel

Marking

Urine marking is far more a male than a female behaviour and occurs more in dominant males, so castration has been used to counter it. For about a third of dogs this has been found to be quickly effective, but a further fifth gradually start again, and half are unaffected.

Rubbing dogs' noses in their excrement, or punishment after the event, is counterproductive, especially for fearful dogs. If the dog is seen in the act of fouling, a sharp 'uh' sound can halt proceedings.

Change of diet can trigger fouling and flatulence, particularly in older dogs and flat-faced breeds. Some breeds can also be more problematic with house-soiling, such as Beagles and excitable Toy breeds, such as Yorkshire Terriers, that were selected for their pup-like behaviour.

To establish the pattern of fouling, keep a diary: record not just when incidents occur, but also times of walks, whether the dog relieved himself, diet changes, stressful events and so on. From this you can see whether feeding times could be different, and whether walks are long enough for the dog.

Eating droppings  82

When owners see their dog eat droppings – faeces – they are understandably disgusted.
They know dogs are scavengers, but surely this is taking scavenging too far!

German Shepherd

Coprophagia has always been understood as normal in bitches with young pups while they are in the nest still in the suckling phase, when she licks up their faeces and urine. When a bitch is still cleaning up her pups' elimination, she is also regurgitating food for them to eat, so inevitably there will be some faecal contamination of their food, which may condition their preferences.

Although wolves are not identified with coprophagia, at a kill they will often rip open the gut and consume it and its contents. It may be this aspect that is missing from the diet of household dogs, and the bacterial gain from coprophagia may compensate.

In adult dogs, apart from observations that it seemed more common in unowned or rescue dogs and that it might arise from hunger, nutritional deficiency, stress or boredom, eating droppings was just viewed as regrettable behaviour for many years.

However, new research by Dr Joanne van der Borg of Wageningen University, Holland, is giving a basis to begin understanding something about the behaviour. From investigating 517 problem dogs she found just over 11 per cent ate dog droppings. What is a step forwards is that she found of these, while 56 per cent ate the stools of other dogs, 37 per cent would eat only their own, while only 7 per cent would eat both those of other dogs and their own. That there are these distinct differences brings the realization that more is involved than just a 'bad habit'. A further finding was that there was no real difference between the sexes when it came to eating their own droppings, but that when it came to eating other species' droppings, significantly more females did this than males.

Dogs on commercially available foods tend to have a more plant-based diet than their more carnivorous forebears, who gave them a carnivore's short gut length. Like herbivores, dogs have bacterial fermentation, helping to break down food in their large intestines and producing fatty acids, thiamine and other B vitamins. It has been suggested that the specific eating of cat droppings, with their high protein content, can supplement the dog's intake.

Because of dogs' history of scavenging and burying food and bones for later consumption in partially decomposed states, taste aversion therapy is not often successful. Dogs not only are used to foul tastes, but have a tolerance of nausea.

SOLUTIONS

- The use of hot pepper or a similar substance put on to faeces your dog is about to eat can cause subsequent avoidance.

- A free-running dog has access to many droppings, so controlling a dog on a lead can be effective during the period of modifying behaviour.

- A muzzle can prevent consumption of faeces.

- Obedience training programmed with clear commands of 'no' can modify behaviour.

Rolling in droppings

'Oh, why have you done that?' so many owners cry out in despair when their clean dog has just rolled his shoulder into a pile of faeces, which has now rendered him intensely and unpleasantly aromatic. Now you have to walk home or, worse, sit with that smell in the car on the way back!

From a biological perspective, dogs are not alone in this habit, for a number of other carnivores rub their necks, shoulders and chin in strong-smelling materials: for example, Spotted Hyenas rub in this way but reserve their most frenzied rolling to their own vomited-up hairballs. For civets, rubbing around on decomposing animal materials is part of both eating and sexual behaviour; rolling on rotting carrion is also behaviour common to a number of wild species of the dog family.

Non-carnivores such as Red Deer Stags make a muddy wallow with their own urine at the height of the breeding period, and roll and saturate their coats in the pungent mud. Even clean-coated, fastidious cats will still roll about in an in-oestrus-like fashion when they rub on a bush of catnip, which has a volatile oil that smells similar to sexual scents.

The usual explanation of why dogs roll in smelly substances is that they are trying to mask their own scent for predatory or social reasons. However, zoologist R.F. Ewer made the point that in the canid family scent-marking organs are not as developed as in some other carnivores, which may be because they have developed more dependence on vocal or

SOLUTIONS

- Watch out for your dog focusing on something smelly on the ground and circling it; at any second the shoulder will drop down, and so will he.
- Anticipate this, and distract your dog with a call.
- If your dog is on a side-head halter, move to the side with a rapid move of a distracting toy.
- Move away from the spot, then command your dog to 'sit', rewarding him when he does.
- Watch out for rotting fish on the banks of a stream, which must be one of the worst smells once it is spread on a dog.

visual signals that can be changed to suit the circumstances more rapidly. This may be why another's strong scents are 'borrowed' at certain times by rolling, and may (by comparison to other species) have a sexual function.

To the dog the smell appears pleasurable, and on occasions when one rolls on droppings or rotting carrion, another, attracted by the activity, will then sniff the material and join in. Part of why it seems pleasurable is that the dog has his mouth ajar as he rolls around, so he may be picking up volatile scents via his Jacobsen's organ, which interprets sexual scents.

When you arrive home with your foul-smelling dog, to avoid matting problems, particularly in breeds prone to this, you should brush out the rest of the coat before washing. If your dog is a regular roller on unpleasant material, you may have to bathe him more regularly than is good for his coat, so use a gentle, fragrance-free shampoo.

We shouldn't be too hard on dogs for this habit; after all, we do exactly the same, putting on strong smells (albeit from bottles) for sexual seduction reasons – and some of the most expensive perfumes used to be based on material exuded from the rear end of civets!

Sealyham Terrier

Unhappy traveller

Cars are a fact of life for the modern dog, and while most dogs enjoy trips, others have problems: some become nauseous with motion sickness, and others find the vehicle intimidating to the point of panic. The key to avoiding these problems is gradual habituation – breaking the experience down into manageable bits to which your dog can become acclimatized.

Get your dog used to being in the car when you are not going anywhere: sit in it with him, and then both go back into your home. On other occasions sit in the car with your dog for a while with the engine ticking over, but going nowhere, then switch off and again go back indoors. Repeat this with short journeys, coming straight back, and then lengthen the journeys. This gradual build-up is useful with wary and excitable dogs, who come to treat the car and travel in a more matter-of-fact and less stressed way.

With dominant dogs who are likely to display possessive behaviour, avoid suggesting an equality of position or an acknowledgement of their dominance by allowing them to leap straight into the car and on to a seat as soon as a door is opened. If you have a vehicle that can take a crate, this is where previous crate training (see page 84) can benefit – the dog will feel secure in his familiar crate and will not be able to leap about, nor can he be destructive (top: Puli and crate).

Miniature Poodle

When your dog is getting into the crate or into the car, instruct him with a command to wait or to sit and stay. It is just as important when your dog leaves the car that he does not bound out excitedly – roadsides and car parks are not safe places for dogs to emerge at speed, plus people in the car can be hurt by an enthusiastic emergee.

If your car is not of a shape to take a crate, most cars can have a dog grill fitted to compartmentalize the car. Your dog can be introduced to this in the same way as a crate. However, if this is also an area that at other times is seating for people, do not allow a destructive dog to sit on unprotected seats – people have feelings too!

An uncaged dog should have a harness with seat-belt attachments. This may take a little getting used to, but in a crash your dog can become a potentially lethal projectile.

Cocker Spaniel (in working clip)

SOLUTIONS

- Avoid exciting your dog too much before getting into the car; it is better for both the dog and your safety if he is calm.
- Dogs should not be left in a car without ventilation and shade from direct sun; large and flat-faced dogs are at particular risk in a hot car.
- Dogs need water and comfort stops, too.

As the period of early association of man and the wolf leading to the emergence of the domestic dog has now been set much further back in time than believed previously, to around 14,000 years ago (and possibly much more), the relationship has had a fair amount of time to mature.

Nepalese puppy

The Russian researcher, Ivan Pavlov, is renowned the world over for his work with dogs' reactions to bells and the conditioned response in salivating dogs in the late 19th century. His work investigates both the gaining and the extinction of conditioned reflexes. At around the same time, via his work with animals in boxes operating levers, Edward Thorndike in the USA investigated learning methods that he interpreted as trial or error.

A pioneer of more recent dog training was Konrad Most, whose book *Training Dogs* was published in 1910 and laid the basis for some behavioural concepts of training. He founded the German military dog's system, and was Director of Army Canine Research until 1937. World War I also saw a wider training of guide dogs for blinded soldiers in Germany.

The changing approach

Traditional control emphasized punishment for 'bad behaviour', which the dog's hierarchical nature accepted, though not without problems. Today's emphasis is on reward, and recognition of the inheritance of wolves' passive rank assertion.

Co-following the herds would bring overlap between men and wolves, but scavenging from carcasses would have brought change. An interdependence would keep particular groups side by side, and over time a genetic slide from the wolf would occur. Yet the biggest change for contact must have occurred when pups were picked up and brought up by people, with the inevitable socialization; and from then on there was even the opportunity for tethering and control. The first written dog manual to come down to us was titled *Cynegeticus* and written by Xenophon, a writer and soldier born in Attica around 435 BC. He wrote of the breeding and management of sporting dogs in remarkable detail.

Training has been a key part of the relationship between man and dog over the centuries, and many training methods were used on this clever species. However, the modern scientific behavioural approach was moved forwards by Charles Darwin's observations on dog expressions and postures in *The Expression of the Emotions in Man and Animals*, published in 1872. C. Lloyd Morgan developed the 'trial and error' idea watching his own dogs.

Border Collie & German Shepherd

Operant behaviour: a system of reward 86

The change from traditional correction-based training to current reward-based training has stemmed from the research of B. F. Skinner, who coined the term 'operant behaviour' in 1937. In essence, behaviour that shows modification is operant – for example, when hunting for food in one area is repeatedly unrewarded, a wolf or pack will change to another area.

Pavlov had instituted a conditioned response to bells for the reflex of saliva production to food; Skinner distinguished an operant response as a piece of behaviour that became reinforced by a reward such as food. Rewards were termed 'positive reinforcers' as they increased the likelihood of the behaviour occurring.

Labrador

In 1951 Skinner wrote about shaping dog behaviour by reinforcing operant behaviour by a clicker device (originally a toy cricket that could be clicked). He then substituted a conditioned response to the clicker to the learned response for food, and the clicker was a 'conditioned reinforcer' (see page 122).

Animal trainers in displays and circus trainers in shows had for years trained dogs and other animals to do complex sequences of novel behaviour, such as one small dog in a toy wheelbarrow being pushed along by a larger dog around a route. Skinner examined and used the technique of shaping each behavioural component individually and adding another, then another into a working chain of novel behaviour, or 'chaining'. Such sequences of behaviour can be achieved by most owners using positive reinforcement techniques (rewards). Food rewards are usually tiny cubes of meat. Rewards can also be praise, patting, giving a favourite toy, or a conditioned reward, such as a click from a clicker.

However, Skinner's ideas stem from the idea of a dog as an 'automaton', and thus do not allow for instinct. Some behaviours are less likely to be changed by conditioning due to the dog's genetic inheritance, such as the desire to chase.

87 The clicker

So what is the clicker? It is nothing magic, just a small strip of flexible metal set in a plastic box; when you press it and then release, it makes the distinctive 'click' of its name. It is a simple, yet very powerful tool in dog training.

Using a clicker, you can easily get your dog to form an association in his mind between the click sound and food treats as a reward. Just get your dog to perform a piece of behaviour you know he will do, such as sit – or if he's not yet trained to do that, just say his name and when he looks at you, click, then treat. Repeat this a few times and your dog will soon make the connection.

The great value of the clicker is its precision. You cannot step forwards with a food treat at the precise point of each piece of wanted behaviour, and even verbal praise takes much longer than a swift click. The advantage of this precision is that your dog can get to know exactly what you want, instead of guessing from a number of options. Most owners who are not experienced obedience trainers use a large number of words while training, and although *we* know what we are saying, your dog does not speak your vocal language and so our instructions lack clarity. With a clicker, your dog will be delighted that you have learned to communicate at last!

An alternative to conventional correction-based training, in which an animal may be scolded for 'bad' behaviour and encouraged for 'good', the clicker is an operant system where specifically 'good' or wanted behaviour is rewarded. The behaviour is shaped in the direction you want purely by positive reinforcement initially of the 'conditioned reinforcer' (the clicker) and then rewarded with a titbit of food or an alternative.

Whether to get a dog to weave around a line of cones or, in the more practical world, for a disabled owner to get a dog to negotiate a particular route to pick up keys from a hook, the clicker principle is the same.

Wait until the dog just happens to approach a cone and starts to go around it, then click. When he approaches another cone in a similar way, click again, then give a treat. You will realize how bright your dog is when he catches on after just a few clicks, but this also depends on your timing and clicking at just the right moment – timing is all! Don't go on too long, and finish each session with hands-on praise.

Clicker training is not only about learning new routines; it can also correct problems by the clicker reinforcing preferred new behaviour. For example, each time a pulling dog eases off and the lead goes slack, click and then treat the dog – within a remarkably short time, the behaviour usually changes. You can start using the clicker with a dog of any age, from a pup to a mature animal – one of the cases where you can teach an old dog new tricks!

Click and reward

If this system is to work it requires some discipline in the owner:
- First, do not use the clicker as a toy or allow it to be used as one by others.
- Second, rapid random clicks without reward will destroy the necessary link in the dog's mind between clicker and reward.
- Finally, don't overuse the clicker – it is primarily for training sessions.

Interrupting or distracting behaviour

During training your dog may have a tendency to become interested in something other than what you want. This can range from following an interesting scent to a small, snappy dog protecting 'his' patch, such as a chair. One general technique that can be usefully employed is to interrupt the established pattern with a distraction.

Dalmatian

One form of distraction consists of commercially available discs that can be carried in the pocket and dropped on the ground when needed. A bunch of keys can work just as well. Alternative sound effects can be made by rattling a few coins in an empty plastic water bottle, thin cloth or plastic bag. (One advantage of these is that with care the noise can appear not to come from the handler; however, if repeated, most dogs soon make the association.) Once the distraction has been made, the dog should be recalled and restarted on the activity.

More immediately – and often more appropriately – a short, sharp, firm sound made by the owner, such as 'uahh', conveys a distractive noise, in the manner that another dog may make. A quick handclap can have a similar effect.

For more distant distraction, such as when your dog is off the lead and does not wish to return as he is too interested in other things, larger and louder moves are effective. These include making yourself a more interesting feature by running around waving and calling, or lying down and waving, which most dogs will be unable to resist investigating. Whatever distraction you use, a distraction by itself is often not as effective as a distraction followed by allowing or encouraging a preferred or displacing activity, and the timing of rewarding praise is especially critical.

WATER PISTOLS

One method of interruption commonly advocated by behaviourists is firing a water pistol at the dog – this is particularly effective fired towards the back of the head of larger dogs, because if the dog sees you fire, the effect will be more that of punishment (or attack), rather than being an independent distraction. In addition, water pistols have to be placed at strategic positions, and the time spent picking them up means that the precise moment where the distraction would be optimal may be missed. The method can also be problematic with vulnerable or particularly dominant dogs.

'Training' collars sold as 'distracting' give an electric shock or citronellal vapour when a dog barks or approaches a property boundary. As the only reward is when the negative stimulus stops, this makes it more of a punishment than a distraction.

Training classes

If you have not previously successfully trained dogs, you will normally benefit from attending dog training classes. Experienced dog trainers will be able to ensure you and your dog reach a good standard, but the most important requirement is for you to establish a proper and good relationship with your dog and work from an understanding of his needs.

Border Collies & Black Mongrel & Yellow Labrador

Pem... Corgi, W... Boxer, Mongrel

Puppy classes can be a real boon to enhance early socialization: if your pup had been born in the wild, he would still have been dashing about with littermates for some weeks after the time you took him home. You should be training your pup some basic moves at home as described in this book, then when he is old enough he can attend a basic level obedience class, usually run by an experienced dog trainer in your area. Such classes are as much about giving owners a proper idea of how to position themselves with their dogs so that the dogs know what their owners want, as to training the dogs – you learn as a team.

Particularly when you start, do not become dispirited if you find your dog responds better to the trainer than to you. A dog's response is as much about understanding the handler's intent as it is about the dog learning moves, and the trainer will have the confidence to convey intent clearly. As you gain experience, you too will gain confidence and your dog will respond better.

However, as classes tend to be weekly, they can only provide a limited input and ensure that you are progressing in the right direction: a good trainer will quickly spot what you are doing wrong – or right! The responsibility for proper training is entirely down to you, so for the rest of the week you have

to put in the work. Once you have achieved a good standard for what you require, you can then cut down your classes to once a month; the benefit of continuing is that it keeps both of you with a training focus, rather than becoming lazy, forgetting about training or drifting into bad habits.

If you find you really enjoy working with your dog and want to do more than learning the basic moves, then look for more advanced classes and groups, which can offer you the opportunity to specialize in agility, tracking, display work or other competition possibilities.

MAKING A START

You can find information on local dog training clubs and classes in the phone directory, via the Internet, from your vet, through the Kennel Club or via a dog trainer's organization who will recommend a local group.

Talk to other dog owners and find out their experiences; go along to the classes and sit in without your dog, so you can see whether the club or trainer is one you like.

Look at a number of classes if possible, before making any decisions: reputable trainers will not take offence and will more likely be pleased you are taking the trouble on your dog's behalf.

Today, breeds that were developed as gundogs are mainly kept as family pets, and as such are trained to those needs, or perhaps for competitive obedience showing or agility competitions. However, some are trained to their original use, although these dogs may not subsequently settle well to family life. Owners requiring working gundogs more usually select from proven working lines that have had success.

Working dogs understandably require specialist training, or training with particular emphasis, usually available with a local gundog society, the address of which can be obtained from the Kennel Club. For example, one of the most important requirements of a gundog that is intended to work in the field or in field trials, is that he should sit on command, even though his instincts tell him to chase.

Experienced gundog trainers gently train puppies under six months with the practical control commands, such as sit, heel or enter water, and only begin more intense training after that age.

Different roles

As different working gundogs were developed for very different roles, after general training they have naturally diverged in their specialist training. For example, quartering for game involves systematically going in one direction for 25 yards, and then back the other way on command, investigating the cover while doing so. The historic and working role of a spaniel is to methodically seek game, then by quartering to push game up, then to completely stop and not to follow the game; because of the limits of a shotgun's range, the spaniel's activities must stay within 25 yards of the gun.

Working retrievers, however, are not taught the specialist spaniel technique of pushing up or quartering; and in further contrast, pointers and setters don't retrieve, but are trained to seek out game in a way that is not dissimilar to quartering by spaniels – the big difference is that they should not flush out birds before the guns arrive but instead should slow down, crouch and point in the direction of the birds.

Springer Spaniel

The advent of dog showing, rather than dogs being worked, as in the past, has led to a wide range of inheritable disorders in dogs. Today there are no common breeds without inherited problems: large dogs, such as German Shepherds, are prone to hip dysplasia; dogs with flapped ears, such as Bassets and Cocker Spaniels, are prone to excess wax and ear infections; Cavalier King Charles Spaniels and Doberman Pinschers are prone to heart disease; British Bulldogs have many problems, and so on.

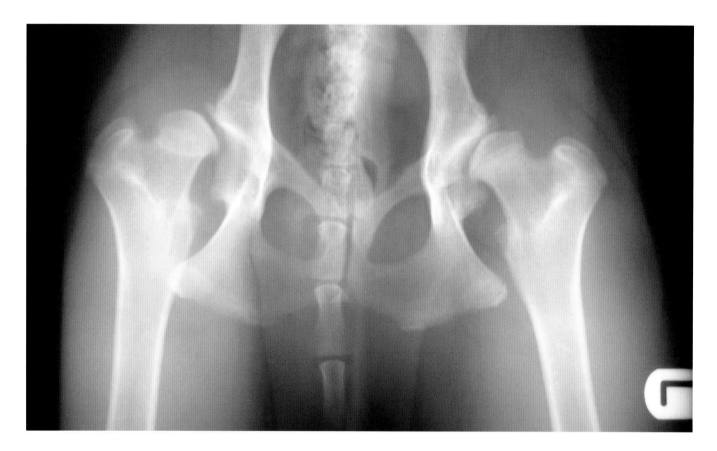

Breeds that have been selected for their large size are naturally more vulnerable to stress and strain on muscles, bones and joints. The ball and socket joints of the hips of large dogs, including German Shepherds and Labradors, can degenerate, causing pain and in extreme cases the inability to walk. In the 1970s the British Kennel Club and British Veterinary Association introduced the idea of scoring hips for severity of abnormality by taking X-rays of dogs over a year old, with a range of 0–53 for each joint. This system is now widely used, and it is advisable not to breed from dogs with a higher score than the breed average. A hip score is not just to inform breeders; it also allows individual owners to plan an exercise and feeding programme, which can significantly reduce the amount of damage. Owners need to be cautious, as dogs are good at hiding their pain, but dogs on painkillers should not be walked vigorously, as this can be damaging.

Elbow dysplasia is the development of damaged cartilage in the elbow joint, which again affects larger dogs, including Great Danes, Newfoundlands, English Mastiffs, German Shepherds, Labradors, Golden Retrievers and Bernese Mountain Dogs. There is a grading system in place for elbow problems.

Not all problems are a direct genetic inheritance, such as a modified enzyme – they are often the result of a genetic selection for a factor such as size; in elbow and hip dysplasia, both genetic and environmental factors may be involved. One form of elbow dysplasia, osteochondritis dissecans, arises from a disruption of the arrival of oxygen and nutrients to the elbow during growth. It is common in Labradors and Golden Retrievers, and another form occurs in large dogs such as German Shepherds.

In terms of build changes, short-legged Dachshunds, Basset Hounds and Pekingese are prone to slipping discs. Dachshunds also have a tendency to diabetes, along with Poodles and Cavalier King Charles Spaniels, while Dachshunds and Poodles tend towards obesity, as do Labradors and Cocker Spaniels. The popularity of Labradors means they are more commonly seen as obese dogs visiting veterinary surgeries.

Genetically inherited eye defects are relatively common, and dogs with these should not be bred from. Progressive retinal atrophy is a disease where blood vessels to the retina die, causing the consequent loss of function in areas of the retina, and while Labradors and Golden Retrievers have a tendency to lose central area vision, breeds such as Dachshunds, Poodles, English Springer Spaniels and Irish Setters may lose total vision with this condition.

Both Collies and Shetland Sheepdogs can carry the congenital disorder Collie eye anomaly, which also damages the retina. While only 6 per cent of dogs with this go blind in an eye, a disconcertingly high proportion of Collies and Shetland Sheepdogs have the condition, making it the commonest canine eye disease in the UK. Unfortunately, its manner of inheritance means that dogs with normal eyes can give birth to affected pups, but thankfully it can be detected at that stage (DNA tests can identify some genetic problems).

Rough Collie

Golden Retriever & German Shepherd

Behaviour

Some inherited problems are specific behaviour problems: solid-coloured (one-coloured) Cocker Spaniels are prone to displaying rage syndrome, while some Cavalier King Charles Spaniels show a type of psychomotor epilepsy, where they seem to snap their jaws at imaginary flies.

The eyes of flat-faced breeds, such as Pekingese, are vulnerable to being knocked out of the supporting bone orbit by trauma, or even by the dog being picked up by the scruff of the neck, as the eyes are less deeply embedded than in most dogs. Dogs that have been bred and selected over the years for shorter, flatter faces are more likely to encounter respiratory problems, as the soft palate becomes disproportionate in size and can block the larynx.

A breed too far?

The British Bulldog cuts to the heart of the matter of bred-in problems. The history of selective breeding, up until the advent of showing, registration and breeding restrictions, was a much more ad hoc affair. What was important was a dog that could do the job, and a bit of breeding and selection admix here or there was seen as good if it brought what was required to the working end product.

Today most people find the idea of setting one animal on to another to be abhorrent. Yet in England in the mid-18th century it was very common at fairs and events, and butchers could be fined if a bull was not baited before killing it. (Bull baiting was outlawed in the Cruelty to Animals Act of 1835, and had effectively stopped by 1840.)

It is clear that dogs set on to bulls were far from uniform in appearance, but they tended to be selected for strength, agility (to escape the horns) and an undershot jaw to give a locked grip. They were such brave and fearless animals that the 19th-century caricature of John Bull fused with the dog, creating the tenacious 'British Bulldog' image of the British people – during World War II, the stocky, round-headed dog became the nation's icon at times of danger, and Prime Minister Winston Churchill's resemblance to a Bulldog was exploited by everyone from cartoonists to himself.

Although the function that had brought the breed into existence ceased before dog showing took off, the breed was radically changed once it became a show-bench animal. Showing fulfils many positive functions in promoting dogs but carries within itself terrible risks that were not there in the selection process for the original working dog's conformation.

Once a written description sets the standard with a feature such as the Bulldog's large head, and judges award points on that basis, it is inherent that the system will continually push for extreme and exaggerated forms of features. Unless that mathematical inevitability is acknowledged and properly compensated for by going to type, this can lead to genetic problems. Combine that with breeding to the pedigree line with avoidance of outcrossing for proper conformation, and it is not surprising that the modern British Bulldog has changed so much from its active ancestors. Selecting for function as well as appearance had kept a vitality in the breed, which is in danger of being lost as the original function is no longer needed or fulfilled.

19th century British Bulldog

THE BULLDOG TODAY

Most people have a soft spot for the British Bulldog, but things have gone so far that most pups not only have to be born by Caesarean section, but even to get the dogs to mate generally needs determined human assistance (up to three people). Adults can have problems of elbow dysplasia, and patellar dysplasia should be screened ahead of breeding. 'Cherry eye' is common.

The most noticeable problem is that as a flat-faced breed, the British Bulldog has respiratory problems with noisy breathing from its inherited floppy soft palate. The inconvenience of the snoring noise made by Bulldogs and other flat-faced (Brachcephalic) breeds becomes more concerning where significant effort or hot weather or nasal discharge can cause a crisis. Such dogs can die of asphyxia.

Just as we allowed Bulldogs and other breeds to become disadvantaged during the 20th century, with the new perspective of the 21st century we should breed to restore their well-being.

The classic example of a historic type of working sporting dog that sustained a required combination of function and appearance is the decoy dog. This has never been a breed in the modern show-bench sense, but it was little different in its breeding and selection from other sporting dogs, such as the spaniels.

Decoy

The origin of 'decoy' is not that of a stooge luring others to follow; instead, it is an abbreviation of the Dutch 'ende-kooy', which means 'the duck cage'. Decoy ponds were developed in Holland to trap wild duck, and were introduced to Britain in the 17th century. Although decoys once provided birds for the table, today they are used to ring birds for migration studies.

English Decoy Dog

The key feature of the decoy pond is the decoy dog. The decoy pond is a shallow pool with curved, radiating arms that make it look like a turning star from above. The decoy gained its name 'duck cage' from the netting that was strung on decreasing-sized hoops over the pond's arms or 'pipes'. On the bank along the curved sides of the pipes are screens made from reeds, but instead of making a continuous fence, they are staggered to appear continuous from the pond, but in reality have gaps with low screen dog-leaps across them.

When enough duck have landed on the pond the decoy man and dog position themselves out of sight behind the screen nearest to the main pond and the ducks. The decoy man silently signals to the decoy dog, who trots along behind the screen and leaps over the low screen into the full sight of the ducks.

If the dog ran towards the ducks they would take off, but he has been trained to run away from them in front of the next screen into the pipe and then disappear from sight by hopping back over the next low leap. He then circles behind the screen and leaps back into view, again going away from the duck.

Decoy men have always chosen small, light, 'red'-coloured, foxy-looking dogs, and say that this foxy look is essential. It seems that the duck are bemused that this arch-predator of duck is running *away* from them, and, intrigued, they begin to follow into the pipe.

The decoy dog gradually moves down the pipe circling the screens, with the duck following further down the netted pipe. When they are fully in, the decoy man steps out into view and startles the duck down into the keepnet at the end of the pipe.

The working of the decoy pond with the dog may seem improbable, but from first-hand working with one of the last few experienced decoy men, Tony Cook in England's Fenlands, I can confirm that it does work remarkably well and that the ducks do follow the decoy dog.

6

Dogs and us

Black
Labrador 'pup'

Inappropriate choices

The commonest cause of death of dogs under 18 months of age is euthanasia, and the main reason for this is 'behavioural problems'. This frightening reality means we are choosing by default to kill more dogs than are killed by illness, traffic or any other reason, usually because we cannot deal with a problem that we have created.

Great Dane

Problems arise from people making inappropriate choices: for instance, a single woman with young children choosing a large dog such as a German Shepherd for protection without realizing that for the safety of her children, the dog must recognize her as dominant. Similarly, a couple of professionals who work long hours should not even consider choosing a large, active dog, such as a Husky, to be confined for most of the day in their pristine apartment, as the bored dog will trash it.

Making a choice

Because we regard dogs as family members, when making a choice of dog we should not just go on a single criterion, such as 'He looked cute!', 'I needed protection' or 'I felt sorry for him.' There is a choice: get it right, and that family member will be with you and your family for the next decade; get it wrong, and you will be rejecting it sooner rather than later.

One 'breed' often overlooked is the mongrel. While you may not know exactly what you are getting with a mongrel, unlike a pedigree, what you do know is that the excellent out-crossed genetic heritage of the mongrel will probably have fewer inherited problems. However, the reason why a number of mongrels have behaviour problems is that they are often obtained as rescue dogs from shelters. Such dogs can be a problem in young families, and although a potential owner may wish to help an abandoned dog, they should not do so at the expense of the safety and well-being of their own children and family. If you wish to obtain a dog from a shelter, you should have thorough discussions with the staff concerning the appropriateness of any choices.

Alaskan Malamute

Whether they are rescue dogs or have been selectively bred, large dogs are just not appropriate for small houses or apartments, especially ones that are shared with small children or older people, who may not be able to avoid a large, exuberant dog. Before making a choice based on the dog's colour or the prettiness of a particular face or soulful eyes, the potential owner should make an audit of his or her own life to see how the range of choices should be restricted, for everyone's benefit.

Do you, the potential owner, have a suitable garden for the type of dog you would like, in terms of size and activity level of the breed? Should you have a male, as there can be dominance issues with males? Is your property close to others, as some dogs are prone to excessive barking and watchdog barking?

Large dogs are very expensive to feed, and a big dog may eat over 20 times the amount eaten by a toy dog. Veterinary care can be expensive: large breeds tend not to live as long as smaller breeds, and some large dogs have a tendency towards hip problems.

You also need to be realistic about how much time you are prepared to spend every day on extensive grooming, such as that needed by Afghan Hounds, for instance.

Dominant and aggressive breeds

Some dominant breeds, such as the Afghan, can be hard to train, and it may be better to avoid others that have a reputation as an aggressive breed or were selected to be aggressive for their work role. For example, there has been a long debate over Pit Bull Terriers being classified as dangerous dogs; however, if genetically selected sheepdogs have a good ability to herd sheep, it is hard to make a case for dogs that have been selected as fighting dogs being chosen as family pets.

The Neapolitan Mastiff is a wonderfully dramatic dog, but is unbelievably large and has a fighting background. The Japanese Tosa Inu was selected to fight to the death. Even the Shar Pei was the Chinese Fighting Dog, and although it is now bred to reduce its aggressive tendencies, the process is not complete.

Some dogs, such as the English Bull Terrier, Alaskan Malamute, German Shepherd and Japanese Akita, have a reputation for attacking or fiercely fighting other dogs. If you do take on such dogs, you need to anticipate issues of dominance within the household , as well as the safety aspect. Similarly, some dogs have a high tendency to snap at children, including the Pomeranian, Chow Chow and West Highland White Terrier.

Neapolitan Mastiff

Why we choose dogs

Numerous surveys reveal that the key reason people give for owning a dog is companionship. In this the dog holds a mirror to our souls, for over half of owners are emotionally dependent upon their dogs.

In one study that mapped family relationships, over a third of dog owners said they had a closer relationship with their dog than any other member of their family. So despite being another species, some of us don't just think our dog is part of our family, we think it's the best part!

A survey by the American Kennel Club in 2006 reported that a third of women dog owners thought 'If my dog was a man, he'd be my boyfriend', and two-thirds of dog owners would not date someone who didn't like their dog. But putting the dog first in this manner can cause problems, and 14 per cent of dog owners admit that their partner is jealous of their dog – the main reason given was spending so much time with the dog, but some said it was because the dog liked them better than their partner.

For parents, obtaining a canine companion for our children is important, and households with children over 6 and under 17 are most likely to seek a dog. An Australian study found that owners felt that a primary reason to have a dog, apart from companionship and pleasure, was protection; three-quarters of the owners felt they needed a dog for this reason, and thought the dog protected their home from burglary.

Miniature Pinscher

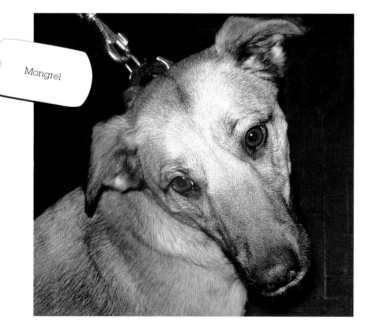

Mongrel

TOP DOG

When we do choose a dog, which is it? Other than mongrel and non-registered breeds, whose popularity fluctuates, for Britain, the USA, Canada and New Zealand, the Labrador is definitely the number one choice. In a number of European countries, the Labrador is just pushed out of that slot by the German Shepherd.

For anyone wanting to see a significant part of the huge diversity of dogs, a championship dog show is where they can be seen, pampered and on display. If you are thinking of owning a particular breed, you will not only be able to see the dogs but also ask questions of the breeders.

When the Kennel Club was established in 1873, standards of breeds became regularized, and breeds were then able to compete within themselves as opposed to previous open competitions, in the manner of open pet classes today. A real interest grew in the idea of types of dog, and just over a hundred years ago, Charles Cruft started what is the largest dog show, and which still bears his name. Each year it runs across four days, with different days for different dog group showing and Agility, Flyball and Obedience events. The 2005 Crufts had 24,000 dogs on show, and afterwards 10 tons of dog poo were carted away!

America's most prestigious dog show, the Westminster Kennel Club show, was started in New York in 1876, and is held annually at Madison Square Garden. Local dog shows attract great numbers of people and dogs, and are used as stepping stones to the national events.

Competitive obedience gives an incentive to improve your dog's level of excellence. Two dog sports are still relatively young, but have a large following – Agility and Flyball – and the breed that excels at both is the Border Collie, which is in essence more a working dog than a pedigree show dog.

Border Collie

AGILITY

The object of Agility events is to compete at the negotiation of different obstacles in a set order within a time limit.

The courses have a series of set obstacles: in addition to hurdles there are a pipe tunnel and a collapsed tunnel to push through, a 'footbridge' to go up, along and down, a vertical tyre to leap through, and a slalom of 12 fairly close upright rigid posts.

FLYBALL

This event was invented in the late 1970s in California.

There are four dogs in each relay team, and there are four hurdles in line down a track. The first dog rushes down the track, leaping the hurdles, and lands on an angled, spring-loaded box that shoots out a tennis ball. The dog grabs the ball and goes back over the start line, when the next dog can follow.

Dog welfare

We all have responsibility for our dogs, and ensuring that we can control them properly is part of that. Caring for their health and well-being is important, and regularly walking and training them, and treating them appropriately is all part of ensuring they don't become part of the statistics on abandoned dogs.

SOLUTIONS

Before taking any adult shelter dog home, do a behaviour test to reduce the risk of having to return him. If he responds to any of these tests below in such a way as to give concern, think long and hard as to whether this is the appropriate dog for your home, and be realistic – for the dog's sake as well as your family's.

- With the dog on a lead, approach him and see if he is wary.
- See if he responds to the basic command 'sit'.
- Ask for another dog on a lead to be brought near, and watch the dog's response.
- Ask for the dog to be left alone in an office for 10–15 minutes to see if he remains OK.

A visit to any dog shelter can be heart-wrenching: although it is always pleasant to see dogs, and the staff and volunteers ensure that they are well cared for, the sheer number of dogs that go through shelters is a real measure of our failure as a society to care for our canine companions.

About 15,000,000 animals go through the world's biggest dog-owning country's shelters annually. Of dogs going into shelters in the USA, 56 per cent are euthanazed, 25 per cent are adopted, and only 15 per cent are reunited with their owners after being lost.

One of the commonest reasons dog owners give to shelters for relinquishing a dog is 'moving', claiming that it would not be possible to keep them at the new home. The National Council on Pet Population Study & Policy found that dogs were more likely to be relinquished to a shelter if they were sexually intact, had been obtained for free, were over six months old when obtained, and had turned out to be more work than expected by the owner. From this it can be seen that unreasonable expectations of what owning a dog entails were a strong feature behind dog rejection.

Collars and chips

More pets would be reunited with their owners if the owners made sure that not only their dogs wore a collar, but that this has the owner's current contact details. Microchips or a tattoo should also be there, for collars and tags do get lost; however, don't rely purely on a microchip, as a chip reader has to be available before anyone knows how to contact you. In the UK around 100,000 stray dogs are currently dealt with a year by dog wardens and others for local authorities, and over half are reunited with their owners.

Obesity: dogs at risk 97

Unfortunately we are in the midst of a canine obesity 'epidemic'. As long ago as the early 1970s 20–44 per cent of dogs were being classified as obese, with excessive body fat impairing body function; and things have not improved since then. All too often, other issues such as reward and affection have become conditionally linked to food.

Obesity in dogs is a reflection of the growth of human obesity in the West, currently led by the USA but closely followed by the UK and continental Europe. Morbidly obese individuals are often in denial of the all-too-simple reasons of insufficient exercise and excessive intake of food. 30 years ago it was found that obese owners were twice as likely to have obese dogs than non-obese owners; even today, a third of owners of obese dogs do not acknowledge that their dogs are overweight.

We clearly should not put our dogs' lives at risk, or cause them the problems of ill health by making them overweight. However, if our reward systems are conditioned to food reward, treating our pets is an inevitable extension. Over 60 per cent of owners give their dogs treats, and over half give food from the table in addition to the dog's own food. Ironically this is the very basis of the operant reward training methodology, which is why the food rewards of training are very small, and substituted with other rewards.

The medical risks are real: obese dogs are much more likely to suffer from diabetes mellitus, orthopaedic problems, arthritis, cardiovascular disease, breathlessness and other problems. When weight-linked, these risks haven't just happened – we have caused them, for we give dogs their food and control its quantity, whether too little, too much, or 'just right'. One key factor is portion size, and all too often that is where the 'affection factor' kicks in.

Certainly in the majority of cases obesity arises from too much intake of food, or too little 'burn off' by exercise. In the UK 25 per cent of owners admit they don't exercise themselves or their dogs. In the USA 25 per cent of dog-owning households are multi-dog, and dogs can become competitive eaters at mealtimes.

Some breeds are more likely to put on weight than others, and owners need to be especially careful with the feeding regimes of Labrador Retrievers, Basset Hounds, Beagles and Cavalier King Charles Spaniels. Be careful of breeds with a vulnerability towards hip dysphasia gaining too much weight. In addition, while gaining weight can lead to damage and medical conditions, the reverse can also occur.

Inherited genetic problems that can affect mobility or give pain, such as hip dysphasia, osteoarthritis, cruciate ligament problems and so on, can reduce the ability for exercise and so predispose a dog towards obesity. Neutering can affect the dog's endocrine system, and lead to weight gain.

The good news is that, according to a 14-year study conducted by an American pet food manufacturer, keeping your dog to his optimal weight is likely to increase his life expectancy by as much as 15 per cent.

Consult your vet

If you put your dog on a diet, especially if it is a small-built breed, consult your vet to avoid a too-rapid weight loss that itself can cause problems.

Fouling and dog parks

Our attitudes towards dogs are changing, not least in reaction to statistics such as the current number of owned dogs in the USA (65 million) allied to Alan Beck's figures for the average dog producing 0.34kg of faeces a day – which makes 22,100,000kg of faeces deposited across the USA a day, or 8,000,000,000 kg per year!

Although most of the public reaction against dog-fouling is probably based on annoyance at stepping into it on the pavement, this is largely justified by the public health argument, based on the risk of Visceral Larva Migrans infection to young children when they eat dirt (usually between the ages of 2 and 5). Responsible owners now carry pooper-scoopers or bags on a roll.

An extension of the debate was started with the creation of dog parks (there are now 700 in the USA). These are usually off-leash, which is more fun for a well-trained dog, and while successful in some areas, these parks have caused problems in some communities.

Dogs are most likely to defecate when off the lead when they are with their owner in urban parks. The density of faeces has been found by researchers to be lower in such public places when dogs are kept on their leads. Consequently, off-leash parks have strong opponents, particularly among mothers of small children and others concerned over the mess and distinctive aroma when walking among dog faeces. In San Francisco the issue has been very heated between groups for some years, while a Seattle Parks Department spokeswoman called her city's experience with off-leash parks 'wildly successful'.

A greater collaboration between dog off-leash groups and park authorities can help, not just in the provision of 'dog-loo' areas and having these regularly cleaned and monitored, but a greater incorporation of behavioural understanding. (In Britain the first Council park to install a 'dog-loo' was appropriately Barking in East London.) The siting of the 'dog-loo' should be in the on-leash approach to the open area of the park.

Basset Hound

VISCERAL LARVA MIGRANS

This condition is caused by roundworms (nematodes) shed from dogs and cats as microscopic eggs in the faeces; the commonest in dogs is *Toxocara canis*. The eggs are not infectious in the faeces, but become so in the soil over weeks and months. Infection is relatively common, infecting 2–10 per cent of children in the USA. The larvae wander through tissues, including the brain and heart, and in rare instances they can damage the retina, causing partial or complete loss of vision in that eye. Fortunately, death has occurred only very rarely.

Pups are often born infected from their mother, and their growth can be retarded. To prevent this, both young pups and their mothers need anthelmintic drugs prescribed on veterinary advice.

It is vitally important that faeces do not contaminate soil anywhere that children have access – not just in public parks, but also in gardens. To further reduce any risks, you should additionally train your dog to use an area from which children are excluded.

Time and motion

Dogs commonly defecate within 20 minutes of eating, and owners can anticipate the timetable; dogs on high-fibre diets will defecate more than those fed on food that is more absorbed during digestion.

Confining a dog to a house when you also have a garden is not taking advantage of the stress relief a garden brings. Even with regular walks, large dogs in particular are likely to go a little 'stir-crazy', but they are more content when allowed outside to a wider range of stimulation.

Golden Retriever

If you do not want the enriching of your dog's life to be entirely at the expense of your enjoyment of your garden, it is important that you train your dog to use one dedicated part of your garden as a latrine. This can be a ringed-off area of grass that is not mowed short, or a dug sandpit (but it is essential that young children cannot use this, so it should be partitioned off from their use). Do not allow faeces to remain in place, and dispose of them appropriately.

A common problem for dog owners whose dogs have access to the main lawn is brown or 'burnt' areas in the grass from urine, another reason why training the dog to use the dog latrine is practical. Dogs' urine's high nitrate content acting as too strong a fertilizer is believed to be the cause, and it has been suggested that this effect is more likely with dogs fed on too high a protein diet and with insufficient access to sufficient drinking water.

In a study Allard found that washing the urine off with a daily watering prevented the grass from browning, but without this, colour change was noticeable after a day. He also found that the type of grass made a difference, and that fescues and rye grass were more resistant, while Kentucky bluegrass was vulnerable. So if you are creating the garden from scratch, paying attention to grass-seed selection can make a more dog-tolerant garden.

In a dog access area, shrubs, paved areas and grass give a more robust structure, while vegetable gardens and precious flowers and bulbs should be fenced off, both to prevent the dog from urinating or depositing faeces, and to stop him from digging or scratching up plants and vegetables. Consideration should be given to avoid plants that are toxic to dogs, such as yew, lupin, box, lily of the valley and so on. Enclose rubbish bins away from the dog's access.

DOG-PROOFING

It is essential that the garden is properly 'dog-proofed' with effective fencing and gates with good latches, to avoid your dog getting on to the street, being at risk and possibly endangering others.

Gaps can be pushed through hedges, so mesh fencing should also be in place where you have these. It is also advisable to have a secure dog kennel and run where the dog can be penned for short periods when necessary.

Wire Haired Fox Terrier

The changing relationship

With humans' increasingly erratic lifestyle over the last 20 or so years, the relative levels of cat ownership have increased at the expense of dog ownership, as the demands of regularly walking and tending to the dog have become less easy to meet.

With the increasing fragmentation of home life, the need has grown for many people, particularly children or old people living alone, to have a close companion in their pet dog to confide in and share walks with. For older people in Britain who live in communal homes without their dogs, a charity called 'PAT Dogs' (Pets as Therapy) meets this need, as registered owners and dogs visit homes where old people need canine company. This can lead to a remotivation and enrichment of lives. Other people have sought a different route, and the relatively new job of professional dog walker for the elderly or disabled has caught on.

Yellow Labrador Retriever

However, it has been repeatedly demonstrated that living with a pet is good for you. Cardiovascular risks such as high blood pressure have been demonstrated to be amenable to reduction with pet ownership as stress is reduced.

The exercise both of you get from taking your dog for a walk is helpful, but your relationship with your dog could also affect your survival. If you and your family are stressed by problems with your dog this will do little to lower your blood pressure, so reflect on how the dog-human relationship can be improved. In addition, a study carried out in 1984 by Baum and colleagues showed that patting a dog with which you have a positive bond has a much stronger effect in lowering blood pressure than in patting one with which you do not have a relationship.

GUIDE AND ASSIST DOGS

Guide dogs for the blind really do give a degree of independence, and assist dogs for hearing-impaired and disabled people make a huge difference to how lives are led.

The specialized level of training required by such dogs exceeds that which most pet owners would feel necessary for their own dogs, but shows what can be achieved. In Britain, the Guide Dogs for the Blind training programme has a long-established and successful track record, and organizations such as Dogs for the Disabled and Canine Partners for Independence depend heavily on reward or positive reinforcement training methods, including clicker training (see page 122), which allows the disabled person to continue the dog's training to their specific needs – from picking up fallen keys to assisting with supermarket shopping.

Cocker Spaniel & Yellow Labrador Retriever

The Kennel Club in the UK is the oldest national registration body for breed dogs in the world, and established the groups. The American Kennel Club is the largest in the world, and issues over 900,000 pedigrees a year. National Kennel Clubs also sanction shows and events for dogs in their countries (see pages 32 and 135).

(see pages 32 and 135)

Key:
AKC = American Kennel Club
KC = Kennel Club (UK)

HOUNDS

AKC & KC:
Afghan Hound, Basenji, Basset Hound, Beagle, Bloodhound, Borzoi, Dachshund, Foxhound, Greyhound, Ibizan Hound, Irish Wolfhound, Norwegian Elkhound, Otterhound, Petit Basset Griffon Vendéen, Pharaoh Hound, Rhodesian Ridgeback, Saluki, Whippet.

AKC only:
American Foxhound, Black and Tan Coonhound, Harrier, Scottish Deerhound.

KC only:
Basset Fauve de Bretagne, Deerhound, Elkhound, Finnish Spitz, Grand Basset Griffon Vendéen, Basset Blue de Gascogne, Hamiltonstovare, Segugio Italiano, Sloughi.

SPORTING DOGS AND GUNDOGS

AKC & KC:
Brittany, English Setter, German Shorthaired Pointer, German Wirehaired Pointer, Gordon Setter, Hungarian Vizsla, Irish Setter, Italian Spinone, Pointer, Weimaraner. Retrievers: Chesapeake Bay, Curly-coated, Flat-coated, Golden Labrador, Nova Scotia Duck Tolling. Spaniels: American Cocker, Clumber, English Cocker, English Springer, Field, Irish Water, Sussex, Welsh Springer.

AKC only:
American Water Spaniel, Wirehaired Pointing Griffon.

KC only:
Bracco Italiano, Kooikerhondje, Large Munsterlander, Irish Red and White Setter.

TERRIERS

AKC & KC:
Airedale Terrier, Australian Terrier, Bedlington Terrier, Border Terrier, Bull Terrier, Cairn Terrier, Dandy Dinmont Terrier, Fox Terrier (Smooth and Wire-haired), Glen of Imaal Terrier, Irish Terrier, Kerry Blue Terrier, Irish Terrier, Kerry Terrier, Lakeland Terrier, Manchester Terrier, Norfolk Terrier, Norwich Terrier, Parson Jack Russell Terrier, Scottish Terrier, Sealyham Terrier, Skye Terrier, Soft-Coated Wheaten Terrier, Staffordshire Bull Terrier, Welsh Terrier, West Highland White Terrier.

AKC only:
American Staffordshire Terrier, Miniature Bull Terrier, Miniature Schnauzer.

KC only:
Cesky Terrier.

WORKING DOGS

AKC & KC:
Alaskan Malamute, Bernese Mountain Dog, Boxer, Bull Mastiff, Doberman Pinscher, German Pinscher, Giant Schnauzer, Great Dane, Mastiff, Neapolitan Mastiff, Newfoundland, Portuguese Water Dog, Rottweiler, Russian Black Terrier, St Bernard, Siberian Husky.

AKC only:
Akita, Anatolian Shepherd Dog, Great Pyrenees, Greater Swiss Mountain Dog, Komondor, Kuvasz, Samoyed, Standard Schnauzer.

KC only:
Beaucaron, Bouvier des Flandres, Canadian Eskimo Dog, Dogue de Bordeaux, Greenland Dog, Hovawart, Leonberger, Tibetan Mastiff.

PASTORAL AND HERDING DOGS

AKC & KC:
Australian Cattle Dog, Australian Shepherd, Bearded Collie, Belgian Sheepdog (Groendendael and Tervueren), Border Collie, Briard, Collie (Rough), Old English Sheepdog, Polish Lowland Sheepdog, Shetland Sheepdog, Welsh Corgi (Cardigan and Pembroke).

AKC only:
Bouvier des Flandres, Canaan Dog, German Shepherd Dog, Puli.

KC only:
Anatolian Shepherd Dog, Belgian Sheepdog (Malinois and Laekenois), Bergamasco, Collie (Smooth), Hungarian Kuvasz, Hungarian Puli, Komondor, Lancashire Heeler, Maremma Sheepdog, Norwegian Buhund, Pyrenean Mountain Dog, Pyrenean Sheepdog, Samoyed, Swedish Lapphund, Swedish Vallhund.

NON-SPORTING AND UTILITY DOGS

AKC & KC:
Boston Terrier, Bulldog, Chow Chow, Dalmatian, French Bulldog, Keeshond, Lhasa Apso, Poodle (Standard and Miniature), Schipperke, Shar Pei, Shiba Inu, Tibetan Spaniel, Tibetan Terrier.

AKC only:
American Eskimo Dog, Bichon Frise, Finnish Spitz, Löwchen.

KC only:
Akita, Canaan Dog, Poodle (Toy), German Spitz (Klein and Mittel), Japanese Akita Inu, Japanese Spitz, Schnauzer, Miniature Schnauzer.

TOY DOGS

AKC & KC:
Affenpinscher, Australian Silky Terrier, Cavalier King Charles Spaniel, Chihuahua (Long- and Smooth-coated), Chinese Crested, Havanese, Italian Greyhound, Japanese Chin, Maltese Miniature Pinscher, Pekingese, Pomeranian, Yorkshire Terrier.

AKC only:
English Toy Spaniel, Manchester Terrier, Shih Tzu, Toy Fox Terrier.

KC only:
Bichon Frise, Bolognese, Coton de Tulear, English Toy Terrier (Black and Tan), Griffon Bruxellios, King Charles Spaniel, Löwchen, Miniature Pinscher, Papillon, Pug.

Pyrenean Mountain Dog x St Bernard

ABOUT THE AUTHOR

Roger Tabor, CBiol., MIBiol., MPhil., FLS, MCFBA, is an internationally renowned animal behaviourist, naturalist and biologist. He is a member of the Canine and Feline Behavioural Association, and is Scientific Advisor to Animal Balance, which controls the dog and cat populations of the Galapagos Islands by a humane community-based neutering project. Roger has travelled the world observing dogs, cats and wildlife, and has written and presented many pet and wildlife programmes on television, mainly on the BBC, but also including PBS in the USA. He is an award-winning, best-selling author, and is Chairman of The British Naturalists' Association. Roger is a keen photographer and takes most of the pictures in his books.

BIBLIOGRAPHY

Beaver, Bonnie, *Canine Behaviour: A Guide for Veterinarians*, Saunders, 1999

Coppinger, Raymond, and Coppinger, Lorna, *Dogs: A New Understanding of Canine Origin, Behaviour and Evolution*, University of Chicago Press, 2001

Hart, Benjamin, and Hart, Lynette, *Canine and Feline Behavioural Therapy*, Lea & Febiger, 1985

Lindsay, Steven R., *Handbook of Applied Behaviour and Training, Vol. II*, 'Etiology and Assessment of Behaviour Problems', Blackwell Publishing, 2001

Morris, Desmond, *Dogs: A Dictionary of Dog Breeds*, Ebury Press, 2001

Parker, Heidi; Kim, Lisa; Sutter, Nathan; Carlson, Scott; Lorentzen, Travis; Malek, Tiffany; Johnson, Gary; De France, Hawkins; Ostrander, Elaine, and Kruglyak, Leonid, 'Genetic Structure of the Purebred Domestic Dog' in *Science*, Vol. 304, pp1160–64, 21 May 2004

Scott, John Paul, & Fuller, John L., *Dog Behaviour: The Genetic Basis*, University of Chicago Press, 1965

Serpell, James (ed.), *The Domestic Dog, its Evolution, Behaviour and Interactions with People*, Cambridge University Press, 1995

Trut, Lyudmila N., 'Early Canid Domestication: The Farm-Fox Experiment' in *American Scientist*, Vol. 87, No. 2, pp160–69, March–April 1999

Overall, Karen, *Clinical Behavioural Medicine for Small Animals*, Masby, 1977

Salman, Mo; Hutchison, Jennifer; Ruch-Gallic, Rebecca; Kagan, Lori; New, John; Kass, Philip, and Scarlett, Jane, 'Behavioural Reasons for Relinquishment of Dogs and Cats to 12 Shelters', in *Animal Welfare Science*, Vol. 3 (2), pp93–106, 2000W

I have been helped over the years by innumerable kind people, whose assistance has been incorporated into the production of this book. I cannot possibly hope to thank everyone who has been involved, and I trust those that I do not mention by name will nonetheless know they have my thanks.

My grateful thanks to the Central Essex Dog Training School, Colchester, Crufts, the Kennel Club, the American Kennel Club, Debbie Rijnders and Tinley Advies and Producties, Dr Lyudmila N. Trut and Shepeleva Darya of the Institute of Cytology and Genetics at the Siberian Division of the Russian Academy of Science, Dr Heidi Parker and Dr Elaine Ostrander of the Fred Hutchinson Cancer Research Centre, Washington University, Seattle, Heidi Hardman of Cell Press, Dr Joanne van der Borg of Wageningen University, Holland, Colin Tennant and the Canine and Feline Behaviour Association, the Humane Society of the United States, Chitwan National Park, Nepal, Emma Clifford and Animal Balance on the Galapagos Islands, Christine Kirkman, Tim Collins, APBC, the US Pet Food Institute, the vets and staff of San Francisco SPCA, RSPCA Danaher Animal Home, Seavington Hunt, Great Bentley Dog Show, Dick Meadows and the BBC, Alfresco TV Cardiff, Tatton Park, Philip Wayre and Norfolk Wildlife Centre and Park, Colchester Zoo, Kruger National Park, Longleat Safari Park; and particular thanks to veterinary surgeon Alan Hatch, MRCVS, for his kind help.

My thanks are also due to those who kindly co-operated with their dogs so pictures could be taken for this book, especially those who have contrived to demonstrate behaviour that their normally perfectly behaved dogs would not do! My thanks particularly go to Natalie Potts, John Beton, Harrison and Chelsea, Pam Lindrup, Sarah Verral, Michelle and Toby Gray, Pamela and John White and Tom Thomas; and also to J. Lightly, N. Staines, Mr Matthew, K.D. and C. Ineson, M. Baldry, Jenni Hastings, Sarah Hurr, T. Dunsdon, S. Tearle, Gill Bingham, Sheila Cox, Lynda Davies, Andrew Pratt, Lyn Wiggins, Katrina Spitz, Frances Stone, R. Vincent, J. Holmes, S.C. Spells, Lin Robins, Mrs J. Robinson, S. Alexander, Frank Wood, Mrs Hardy, Janet Woodhead, Mrs. D. Taylor, Mrs B. Jones, Pete and Wendy Garrard, David Chandler, Mr and Mrs Webb, S. Eburne, E.G. Elliott, Debbie Rjinders, B.J. Henderson, I.S. Hughes, P. Batten Jones, Fred Mason, Mrs Webster, Jean Denton, Emma Redrup, B. and S.E. Smith, Mr P. Bush, Margaret Greening, Julie Olley, Rosemary Turrell, J. Stibbs, Marion Brierley, Paula Clarke and Dempsey, Lynn and Margaret Cuthbert, Tessa Proudfoot, Ann Mills, Sarah Verrall, David Ridgewell, Lesley Scott, Joyce Jackl, Lee Beecroft, Deborah Sage, Richard Verrier, Stuart-lee Hurr, Sarah King, Keith Jones, Diane Beaumont, M. Jones, Paula Hunter, S. Moreton, Angela Clark, Caroline Cox, Helen Green, Cara McGuffie and Charles Llewelyn, S. George, Ray Raymond, C. George, Nicola Beavers, Jenny Goff, Nigel Ball and Ciaran Carr, Catherine Carr, Robert and Lisa Murray, Scruffy Wuffy canine beauticians, Maureen Grant, Sissi Meindersma, Josephine Hayes, Ian Harvey, Moira Sixsmith, Gina Stiff, Kay Lundstrum, Jean Howkins, Susan Osborne, Tony Cook and the Wildfowl Trust, S. Harris, Georgie McGuffie, Tina Brett, Ray Johnson, Sarah Rushton, W.A. Cook, Mrs Riley, Esther and Tony Hague, C. Preston, Steve and Julie Mercer and D. Lunt.

My thanks are also due to Angela Weatherley, and to Jane Trollope, Ian Kearey, Jennifer Proverbs and the rest of the David & Charles team. A final special thanks to Liz Artindale for her considerable help and support.

ROGER TABOR, 2006

PICTURE CREDITS

All the photographs in this book were provided by Roger Tabor, except the following:

Kim Sayer, front cover and pages 3, 5 (bottom right); © Dick Meadows, page 6 (top); Getty Images/America 24-7/Ken Weaver, page 63 (main); Liz Artindale, pages 74 (header), 111 (header, top); © Alan Hatch, Veterinary Surgeon page 126 (main)

The publisher has endeavoured to contact all contributors of pictures for permission to reproduce.